GETTING BY
IN
ITALIAN

**A quick beginners' course for
tourists and businesspeople**

Course writer: Bob Powell
Language adviser: Flavio Andreis
Producer: Mick Webb

BARRON'S/Woodbury, New York/London/Toronto
By arrangement with the British Broadcasting
Corporation

First U.S. Edition published in 1982 by Barron's
Educational Series, Inc.

By arrangement with the British Broadcasting
Corporation, 35 Marylebone High Street, London
W1M 4AA.

Portions of the Reference section of this book from *Ital
At a Glance* by Mario Costantino.

All inquiries should be addressed to:
Barron's Educational Series, Inc.
113 Crossways Park Drive
Woodbury, New York 11797

International Standard Book No. 0-8120-2576-8

PRINTED IN THE UNITED STATES OF AMERICA

345   047   987654

Contents

The course...
and how to use it

Getting by in Italian is a five-programme radio course for anyone planning a visit to Italy. It provides, in a short learning period, a basic 'survival kit' for some of the situations typical of a visit abroad.

The programmes

□ concentrate on the language you'll need for 'getting by' in some of the most common situations – buying food and drink, getting somewhere to stay, finding the way, travelling around, etc

□ include real-life conversations specially recorded in Italy

□ encourage you to develop a good accent, by giving the opportunity to repeat new words and phrases

□ suggest short cuts to learning what you need to say and ways of getting the gist of what's being said even if you don't understand every word.

The book includes . . .

□ the key words and phrases of each programme unit

□ the texts of the recorded conversations in the order they'll be heard in the programmes

□ simple explanations of the language used

□ background information worth knowing about Italy and Italian customs

□ self-checking exercises for you to do between programmes, and a short test on the whole course

- a reference section containing a short pronunciation guide, extra language notes and vocabulary; numbers, days of the week, and months of the year; weather terms; menu items; road signs; useful addresses; and the key to the exercises.

- *Panic stations!* at the end of the book with words and expressions for use in emergencies

The two cassettes contain the radio programmes in slightly shortened form plus pronunciation exercises,

To make the most of the course

The routine you follow depends a lot on you and on whether you're using the cassettes or the radio programmes, or both. Here are a few suggestions:

- Get used to the sounds of the language by listening to the programmes without looking at the book. Some people concentrate better by shutting their eyes.

- When there are words and expressions to repeat, try and say them boldly and clearly.

- After each programme, work through the explanations and exercises, and if possible practise the conversations with a friend. (You could try recording your own voice to check your pronunciation.)

- Learning a language needs plenty of constant practice – a good rule is 'little and often', rather than all at once.

- Be selective about the words you learn – what you're going to say is more important than what other people might say to you.

- When you go to Italy, don't forget to take this book with you, plus a good pocket dictionary.

Coraggio . . . e buon viaggio!

1 Ordering and paying

Key Words

Hello Good morning Good evening	**Ciao Buon giorno Buona sera**
Goodbye 'Bye	**Arrivederci Ciao**
A coffee, please	**Un caffè, per favore**
How much is it?	**Quant'è?**
Thanks – Any time	**Grazie – Prego**
Yes No	**Sì No**
1 2 3 4 5	**uno due tre quattro cinque**

Conversations

These can be heard in the programmes and on the cassettes. New words can be found in the Italian–English word list (page 63).

Helloes and goodbyes

Boy	Ciao.
Girl	Ciao.
Gabriele	Ciao, Massimo.
Massimo	Ciao, Gabriele.
Man 1	Arrivederci.
Man 2	Arrivederci.
Gabriele	Arrivederci, Massimo.
Massimo	Arrivederci.
Customer	Buon giorno.
Shopkeeper	Buon giorno.
Man	Buona sera.
Woman	Buona sera.

Ordering a coffee in a bar

Customer	Un caffè, per favore.
Barman	Un caffè?
Customer	Sì.
Barman	Ecco un caffè.
Customer	Grazie.
Barman	Prego.

ecco   *here is*

. . . a coffee, a cup of tea and a beer

Customer	Un caffè, un tè e una birra.
Barman	Un caffè, un tè e una birra. Il tè con latte?
Customer	Sì, con latte, per favore.
Barman	Ecco il tè.
Customer	Grazie.

. . . a white coffee and a cake

Customer	Un cappuccino e una pasta.
Waitress	Un cappuccino e una pasta?
Customer	Sì, grazie.
Waitress	Prego.

. . . two teas and three coffees

Customer	Due tè e tre caffè, per favore.
Barman	Tre tè e due caffè, signorina.
Customer	No . . . eh, tre caffè e due tè.

Paying for museum tickets

Tourist 1	Due, per favore.
Clerk	Mille lire.
Tourist 1	Mille lire.
Tourist 2	Tre, per favore.
Clerk	Millecinquecento.
Tourist 2	Millecinquecento.

8 otto

Asking how much

Customer	Quant'è?
Barman	Duemila lire.
Customer	Duemila lire . . . ecco cinquemila lire.
Barman	. . . tre, quattro, cinque.

Paying at the cash desk

Customer	Un caffè, una birra, un cappuccino e un latte.
Cashier	Birra estera o nazionale?
Customer	Nazionale.
Cashier	Duemila lire.
Customer	Duemila.

Changing money

Clerk	Vuole cambiare?
Customer	Sì, grazie.
Clerk	Travellers o un assegno?
Customer	Travellers.
Clerk	Il passaporto, per favore.
Customer	Ecco.

Clerk	Grazie. Dove abita?
Customer	Pensione La Residenza.
Clerk	*Firmi qui, per favore. . . . Bene. . . . S'accomodi alla cassa.

vuole cambiare? *do you want to change (money)?*
dove abita? *where do you live?* or *where are you staying?*
firmi qui *sign here*
s'accomodi alla cassa *please go to the cash desk*

Explanations

Saying hello and goodbye

buon giorno literally 'good day' – used like the English 'good morning' or 'morning', but also in the early afternoon

buona sera 'good evening' – used in the late afternoon and in the evening (for 'goodnight', say **buona notte**)

ciao a casual greeting used among friends to mean 'hello – hi there' and also 'bye – cheerio'

arrivederci 'goodbye'

Being polite

per favore 'please'

grazie 'thanks' or 'thank you'; **no, grazie** is 'no, thank you'; 'yes, please' in Italian is **sì, grazie**

prego usually means 'not at all', 'don't mention it', and is an automatic response to **grazie**; it's also used by shopkeepers and barmen to ask 'can I help you?'

s'accomodi usually means 'sit down', but can also be a polite way of directing you elsewhere (eg to the cash desk); **prego** can be used instead

signora, signorina – it's quite normal to address older, married women as **signora** (madam) and younger women as **signorina** (miss); **signore** (sir) is used by shopkeepers etc to address customers, but otherwise isn't very common.

Numbers

0 zero		
1 uno	100 cento	1000 mille
2 due	200 duecento	2000 duemila
3 tre	300 trecento	3000 tremila
4 quattro	400 quattrocento	4000 quattromila
5 cinque	500 cinquecento	5000 cinquemila

1500 millecinquecento 2500 duemilacinquecento

(Sometimes you will hear only millecinque for 1500, or duemilacinque for 2500, etc.)

Masculine and feminine

In Italian, both people and things are either masculine or feminine.

Masculine words usually end in **–o**, eg **passaporto**.
Feminine words usually end in **–a**, eg **birra**.
Words ending in **–e** can be either masculine or feminine, eg **pensione** (fem) and **latte** (masc).

When you come across a new word that you think will be useful, it's worth learning not only the word but also its gender (indicated in most dictionaries by **m** or **f**).

There are two main words for 'a' – **un** and **una**.
Un is used with masculine words, eg **un caffè**.
Una is used with feminine words, eg **una pasta**.
(When a feminine word begins with a vowel, **un'** is used, eg **un'acqua minerale** – a mineral water.)

Exercises

1   Tickets for the museum cost **cinquecento lire** each. Ask for tickets for the following numbers of people.

a   two people   c   four people
b   five people   d   three people

How much will the ticket clerk ask you for each time?

2   Fill in these gaps with the appropriate Italian words:

It's mid-morning and you meet an Italian friend, Gino, in the street. Say hello to him: . . . .

. . . .

You decide to have a drink together and go into a bar. Ask the barman for two coffees – one black and one frothy white: ....
....
You want a cake too: ....
Now ask the price: ....
It's 2000 lire. Offer the barman the right money, and say thank you: ....

3 What do you say –
a If someone offers you a cigarette and you don't smoke?
i Prego. ii Per favore. iii No, grazie.

b If you do smoke?
i Prego. ii Sì, grazie. iii Per favore.

c If someone says **grazie** to you when you've given them a light?
i Prego. ii S'accomodi. iii Per favore.

4 Practise the 'ch' sound in Italian by saying the following words several times out loud. (NB: see *Pronunciation* section, page 54.) Check your pronunciation by listening to the end of Programme 1 on the cassette.

ciao **ci**nque **ci**nema **ce**ntro **ci**ttà **ci**occo**la**ta
cappu**cci**no aran**ci**ata arrive**derci**

5 Look at the section *Drinks and snacks* on page 15. Then try ordering the following items. Say each one out loud in Italian and ask the price each time.

a a coffee laced with **grappa**
b a tea, an Italian beer and a hot chocolate
c an orangeade and a grapefruit juice
d a foreign beer, a toasted sandwich and a roll
e a frothy white coffee and a mineral water

Worth knowing

La banca The bank

Banks are open only in the morning, from 8.30 am until 1.20 pm, Monday to Friday. To change currency look out for the counter sign **CAMBIO**, though you'll probably have to go to a central cash desk **la cassa** to collect your money.

Traveller's cheques are sometimes shortened to **travellers**. An ordinary cheque is **un assegno,** and to cash one under the Eurocheque system you need a cheque card **la carta assegni.** If you need to borrow a pen, it's **una penna.**

Money

The Italian unit of currency is the **lira,** plural **lire.** Banknotes **banconote** come in denominations of 500, 1000, 2000, 5000, 10,000, 20,000, 50,000 and 100,000 **lire**. Coins are mainly 50, 100 and 200 **lire**.

The **lire** sign on price tags is £, the same as we use for the pound sterling. A pound is **una lira sterlina** or just **una sterlina.**

Cafés and bars

Italian bars (a bar is **un bar**) serve both alcoholic drinks and soft drinks, coffee, etc. Most of them also sell snacks and ice-cream.

Sometimes you will have to get the receipt **lo scontrino** at the cash desk before going to the bar itself and ordering. It's quite usual to drink standing at the bar counter – if you sit at a table **al tavolo** you will usually get waiter service and have to pay more for your drinks, sometimes a lot more.

Drinks and snacks

coffee	**un caffè (espresso)** *a small cup of strong black coffee* **un caffè lungo** *slightly weaker, black* **un caffè corretto** *black coffee with a dash of brandy or grappa* **un cappuccino** *white with frothy milk* **un caffelatte** *ordinary white* **un caffè freddo** *iced coffee*
tea	**un tè al latte** *or* **con latte** *tea served with a small jug of milk* **un tè al limone** *lemon tea* **un tè freddo** *iced tea*
chocolate	**una cioccolata** (**calda** – *hot, or* **fredda** – *cold*)
sugar	**lo zucchero**
water	**un bicchiere d'acqua semplice** *a glass of (ordinary) water* **un'acqua minerale** *mineral water, usually slightly fizzy*
beer	**una birra** *either* **nazionale** *(brewed in Italy and of the lager type) or* **estera** *(more expensive foreign brands)*

wine	for different sorts of wines see Chapter 5
soft drinks	**un'aranciata** *orangeade* **una limonata** *lemonade* **un frullato** *milkshake, often made with fresh fruit and ice-cream* **un succo di frutta** *fruit-juice* **una spremuta** *fresh fruit-juice* **– di limone** *lemon* **– di arancia** *orange* **– di pompelmo** *grapefruit*
fancy cake	**una pasta**
bun	**una brioche** *(pronounced 'bree-osh')*
roll	**un panino**
toasted sandwich	**un toast** *(pronounced 'tost')*

2 Shopping around

Key words

Buying an ice-cream	**Un gelato, per favore**
100 grams of ham	**Un etto di prosciutto**
Some cheese	**Un po' di formaggio**
A kilo of peaches	**Un chilo di pesche**
This one	**Questo**
6 7 8 9 10	**sei sette otto nove dieci**
10 stamps for England	**Dieci francobolli per l'Inghilterra**

Conversations

Asking for a mixed ice-cream

Waitress Sì?
Customer Un gelato, per favore.
Waitress Abbiamo cioccolata, caffè, fragola . . . o misto.
Customer Un misto, per favore . . . un po' di caffè, un po' di fragola, e . . . un po' di questo.

abbiamo *we've got*

Buying 100 grams of ham

Shopkeeper Desidera?
Customer Un etto di prosciutto.
Shopkeeper Crudo o cotto?
Customer Eh . . . questo.
Shopkeeper Ah, cotto allora.

desidera? *can I help you?*
cotto allora *cooked then*

. . . some cheese

Customer	. . . e un po' di formaggio.
Shopkeeper	Quale? Pecorino, gorgonzola?
Customer	Questo.
Shopkeeper	Gorgonzola. Va bene così?
Customer	Sì, va bene.

quale? *which one?*
va bene così? *is that OK?*

. . . eight bread rolls

Shopkeeper	Nient'altro?
Customer	Sì, otto panini.
Shopkeeper	. . . quattro, cinque, sei, sette, otto.

nient'altro? *anything else?*

. . . a kilo of peaches and half a kilo of tomatoes

Customer	Buon giorno.
Shopkeeper	Buon giorno. Desidera?
Customer	Un chilo di pesche e mezzo chilo di pomodori.
Shopkeeper	Nient'altro?
Customer	No, grazie.

. . . ten stamps for postcards to England

Shopkeeper	Sì?
Customer	Dieci francobolli per l'Inghilterra.
Shopkeeper	Per cartoline?
Customer	Sì, per cartoline.
Shopkeeper	Millecinquecento lire.

Choosing a wallet

Shopkeeper	Cosa desidera, signora?
Customer	Un portafoglio, per favore.
Shopkeeper	Ecco i portafogli. Quale le piace?
Customer	Quant'è questo?
Shopkeeper	Undicimila lire.
Customer	No, è troppo.

| *Shopkeeper* | Le piace questo a settemila lire? |
| *Customer* | Sì, prendo questo. |

quale le piace? *which one do you like?*
undicimila *11,000*
è troppo *it's too much*
prendo questo *I'll take this one*

Explanations

What shopkeepers will ask you

Desidera?, mi dica or **prego?** all mean 'can
I help you?'

quale?	*which one?*
nient'altro?	*anything else?*
va bene così?	*is that OK?*

To ask for precise quantities

The main quantities used are the **chilo** (kilo), **mezzo
chilo** (half kilo) and **etto** (100 grams)

un chilo di pesche	*a kilo of peaches*
mezzo chilo di pomodori	*half a kilo of tomatoes*
un etto di prosciutto	*100 grams of ham*
due etti di mortadella	*200 grams of mortadella*

Liquids are sold by the **litro** (litre), **mezzo litro** (half
litre) or **bottiglia** (bottle)

un litro di latte	*a litre of milk*
mezzo litro di vino	*half a litre of wine*
una bottiglia di vino	*a bottle of wine*

A bit of . . .

To ask for some or a little bit of something, you use
un po' di, eg **un po' di formaggio** (some cheese).
'A bit more' or 'a bit less' are **un po' di più** or **un po'
di meno**.

If you don't know what it's called
The easiest thing to do is to point and say **questo**
which means 'this' or 'this one'.

More numbers

6 sei	600 seicento	6000 seimila
7 sette	700 settecento	7000 settemila
8 otto	800 ottocento	8000 ottomila
9 nove	900 novecento	9000 novemila
10 dieci	1000 mille	10,000 diecimila

Plurals

When you're talking about more than one thing, you'll probably have noticed a change in the word ending

un francobollo　but　**dieci francobolli**

(masculine words)

una cartolina　but　**dieci cartoline**

(feminine words)

Words ending in **–e** change to **–i**
un gettone　but　**dieci gettoni**

Words ending in accented **–è** and **–à** don't change
un caffè　　**tre caffè**

Don't worry too much about these endings – people will understand you even if you get them wrong.

Exercises

1　You're buying ice-creams for the family at the ice-cream parlour **la gelateria**. Complete this dialogue by filling in what you would say to the salesgirl.

You	*(you need five ice-creams)* . . . .
	. . . .
Salesgirl	Sì. Abbiamo cioccolata, limone, caffè, fragola.
You	*(four mixed ones, and this one)* . . .
	. . . .
Salesgirl	Da cinquecento o da mille?

20 venti

You	(you'll have the cheaper ones) ....
	....
Salesgirl	Ecco cinque gelati.
You	(give her the correct money) ......
	....

2 You've made a shopping list of the following things. How will you ask for them in Italian?

```
200 grams of cooked ham
½ litre of milk
a bottle of mineral water
6 bread rolls
100 grams of gorgonzola
½ kilo of tomatoes
1 kilo of peaches
a bottle of beer
```

3 Where might you be asked the following questions? Choose from: **un alimentari, una gelateria, una tabaccheria, un bar**.

a Crudo o cotto?
b Al latte o al limone?
c Per cartoline o per lettere?
d Alla fragola o al caffè?

What items would you probably be buying in each case?

4 You are in the **bar-tabaccheria**. How would you ask for the following?

a five postcards
b a stamp for a postcard
c two stamps for postcards to England
d cigarettes and matches
e and, while you're there, a white coffee

5 Practise your pronunciation with these phrases. Check your pronunciation by listening to the end of Programme 2 on the cassette.

a quattro etti di prosciutto cotto
b cinque chili di pesche
c tre litri di latte
d una pizza e mezza minerale
e un cappuccino con zucchero

Worth knowing

Postal services

The post office **(la posta** or **l'ufficio postale)** is open from 8 am to 1 or 1.30 pm, Monday to Saturday. In large towns the central post office is normally open in the afternoons as well. The equivalent of 'Poste Restante' is **Fermo Posta**.

Letterboxes are red or yellow, with the word POSTE on them. There may be separate slots marked PER LA CITTA' (for the city) and PER TUTTE LE ALTRE DESTINAZIONI (for all other destinations), or LETTERE (letters) and ESPRESSI (express letters). Registered letters are **lettere raccomandate**.

Stamps are best bought at the tobacconist's **la tabaccheria** (see below).

Il telefono The telephone

As well as telephone booths, you'll also find public phones in bars and shops with the telephone sign outside. As a rule Italian telephones don't take coins, so to make a call you need a token **un gettone,** which you can get from a machine in the phone booth or from the cash desk of a bar or shop which has a public phone. There are usually dialling instructions in English on the phone.

To make a long-distance call, look for a sign saying TELESELEZIONE or INTERURBANA, and make sure you have a plentiful supply of **gettoni**. There are also special offices (either SIP – pronounced 'seep' – or **Telefoni di Stato**) from which you can make long-distance calls without using **gettoni**.

Shopping

Shops usually open around 8.30 am and shut in the evening around 7 or 8 pm. Everything stops for a long lunch break from 12.30 or 1 pm until 3.30 (or later in summer).

Small change **spiccioli** tends to be scarce, so don't be surprised if you're given sweets, stamps or **gettoni** instead of coins.

La tabaccheria The tobacconist's

Often combined with a bar, this is the place for stamps and postcards **francobolli** and **cartoline**.
You can also, of course, buy cigarettes **sigarette** and matches **fiammiferi**. Look for the blue and white sign.

Alimentari

The local grocer's shop, where you'll usually find a wide range of bread **pane,** cooked meats, cheeses and other provisions.

prosciutto cotto cooked ham
prosciutto crudo cured ham
(eg Parma ham)

kinds of spiced pork sausage

salame

mortadella

Among the many types of cheese **formaggio** are

Bel Paese	*mild and creamy*
gorgonzola	*blue cheese*
mozzarella	*mild cheese of rubbery consistency, used on pizzas*
parmigiano	*parmesan, usually grated on pasta and soups*
pecorino	*made from ewes' milk*
ricotta	*a kind of curd cheese*

Other shops

farmacia chemist's – recognisable by the red cross; if it's shut, there'll be a list of chemists that are open on the door

fruttivendolo greengrocer's – for apples **mele,** pears **pere,** grapes **uva,** etc

gelateria for ice-cream of many varieties, worth trying with a topping of whipped cream **panna montata;** the *gelateria* is often combined with a bar

macelleria butcher's – for beef **manzo,** veal **vitello** and pork **maiale;** any steak is **una bistecca**

pasticceria for cakes **paste** and sweets **caramelle**

pelletteria for leather goods – wallets **portafogli,** handbags **borsette** and belts **cinture**

supermercato standard supermarket

3 Traveling around

Key words

Which way's the cathedral?	**Scusi, il duomo, per favore?**
The road to Siena	**La strada per Siena**
A ticket to Rome	**Uno per Roma**
A bus to the town centre	**L'autobus per il centro**
11 . . . 20	**undici . . . venti**

Conversations

Finding places in town

The cathedral? – Straight on

Tourist   Scusi, il duomo, per favore?
Passer-by   Il duomo? Dritto, dritto, sempre dritto.
Tourist   Sempre dritto, grazie.

The station? – Straight on as far as the Square, then turn right

Tourist   Scusi, la stazione, per favore?
Passer-by   Come?
Tourist   La stazione.
Passer-by   Ah, la stazione. Dritto fino alla Piazza della Libertà e poi a destra.
Tourist   Dritto, la Piazza della Libertà e a destra.

come? *what?*

The post office? – The second on the left

Tourist   Scusi, la posta, per favore?

Passer-by	La posta? Prenda la prima . . . no, la seconda strada a sinistra.
Tourist	La seconda a sinistra, grazie.

prenda *take*

If someone asks you the way . . .

Motorist	Scusi, la strada per Siena?
Foreigner	Sono straniero.
Motorist	Come?
Foreigner	Sono straniero.
Motorist	Ah – grazie lo stesso.

sono straniero *I'm foreign*
grazie lo stesso *thanks all the same*

Catching a train

Buying a single ticket to Rome

Traveller	Uno per Roma.
Clerk	Andata e ritorno?
Traveller	Andata.
Clerk	Seconda classe?
Traveller	Sì.
Clerk	Tredicimila.

Finding the right platform

Traveller	Per Roma?
Porter	Binario numero quindici.
Traveller	Come?
Porter	Binario numero quindici.
Traveller	Bene, grazie.

Catching a bus to the town centre

Tourist	L'autobus per il centro, per favore?
Passer-by	E' questa fermata, il numero quattordici, quindici o sedici.
Tourist	Il numero quattordici, quindici o sedici. Grazie.

è questa fermata *it's this stop*

Explanations

Asking the way

Start with **scusi** (excuse me), then name the place you're looking for, eg **scusi, il duomo, per favore?** (**il** and **la** both mean 'the' – see below)

Understanding directions

They're often complicated, but words to listen for are:

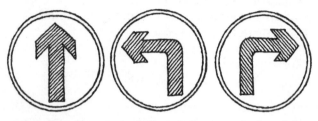

dritto straight on   **a sinistra** left   **a destra** right

la prima strada the first street
la seconda strada the second street

If you don't understand

The easiest way to get something repeated is to say **come?** (what?) or **prego?** (sorry, what?).

If you're really stuck

non capisco	*I don't understand*
sono straniero	*I'm foreign (man)*
sono straniera	*I'm foreign (woman)*
sono inglese/irlandese/ gallese/scozzese	*I'm English/Irish/ Welsh/Scottish*

Buying tickets

Destination

uno per Roma	*one (ticket) to Rome*
due per Londra	*two to London*

Type of ticket
andata/andata e ritorno *single/return*
prima/seconda classe *first/second class*

'The'

There are different words for 'the' – **il, la** or **l'**
il with masculine words **il duomo, il campeggio**
la with feminine words **la stazione, la toilette**
l' with words beginning **l'autobus, l'ospedale**
   with a vowel

Words are given with **il, la** or **l'** in the *Word list.*
You'll also find one or two with **lo** – see *Extra language notes,* page 55.

More numbers

11	undici	16	sedici
12	dodici	17	diciassette
13	tredici	18	diciotto
14	quattordici	19	diciannove
15	quindici	20	venti

Larger numbers are written as one –
often long – word
150 centocinquanta   750 settecentocinquanta
11,500 undicimilacinquecento
13,600 tredicimilaseicento

First, second, third, etc

$1°$ primo $2°$ secondo $3°$ terzo $4°$ quarto $5°$ quinto

Exercises

1   You and a friend are at the railway station in Florence. You can't see the ticket office **la biglietteria,** so you ask a porter to direct you. Fill in your part of the dialogue.

You   *(ask for the ticket office)* . . . .

     . . . .

Porter	Là in fondo a sinistra.
You	*(what? — you didn't catch that)* . . .

. . . .

Porter	A sinistra.
You	*(on the left – thanks)* . . . .

. . . .

Having found the ticket office . . .

You	*(you want two tickets for Pisa)* . . . .

. . . .

Clerk	Andata e ritorno?
You	*(no, single)* . . . .
Clerk	Prima classe?
You	*(you want second class, please)* . . .

. . . .

Clerk	Quattromila lire.

How much change would you expect from a 10,000 **lire** note?

2   Using the map opposite, you're at the Tourist Office **Ente Turismo** and you get the following directions from the clerk. Where would you be going on each occasion?

a   alla Piazza della Repubblica, poi a destra
b   alla Piazza della Repubblica, la prima a sinistra, e poi dritto
c   a sinistra, poi a destra fino alla Piazza Maggiore, e poi a sinistra

Still at the Tourist Office, you're given new sets of directions. You don't catch some of the words, though – what would they be?

d   a . . . . fino a Via Roma, poi a destra – l'ospedale è a sinistra
e   a destra fino alla Piazza della Repubblica, la prima a sinistra, la banca è là in fondo a

. . . .

f   a sinistra, poi a destra fino alla Piazza
    Maggiore, poi ...., la posta
    è là in fondo
What questions did you ask to get the answers
d, e and f?

Key to map

B	Banca Nazionale	P	Posta
C	Campeggio	R	Ristorante Amalfi
D	Duomo	T	Ente Turismo
FS	Stazione	Z	Giardino Zoologico
H	Ospedale di Santa Teresa		

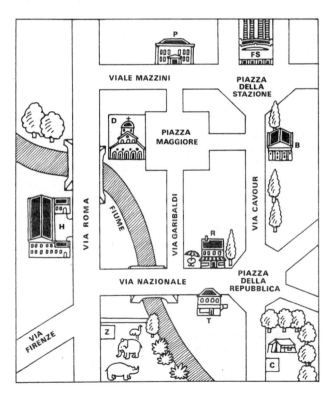

3 Which sign would help you in these situations? (Look at the *Worth knowing* section if you're stuck.)

a trying to find the middle of town
b wanting a toilet
c looking for the cathedral
d finding your way out of an art gallery
e finding your way to the trains after buying your ticket

4 Match these prices to their tickets. Practise saying the numbers out loud – check your pronunciation with that at the end of Programme 3 on the cassette.

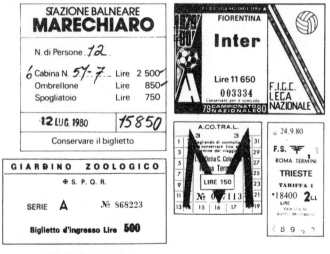

a undicimilaseicentocinquanta lire
b diciottomilaquattrocento lire
c centocinquanta lire
d cinquecento lire
e quindicimilaottocentocinquanta lire

Worth knowing

Getting around

By car

Petrol **benzina** is sold by the litre (five litres = just over a gallon). There are two grades available – **normale** (2/3 star) and **super** (4 star). Ask for **venti** or **trenta litri** (20/30 litres), or a precise amount of money, eg **ventimila lire di super**. To fill up, say **il pieno, per favore**.

Italy has an extensive motorway system but you have to pay a toll **pedaggio** on nearly all sections. The motorways are numbered A1, A2, etc (A for **Autostrada**).

Some useful common road signs

ACCENDERE I FARI IN GALLERIA	*use headlights in tunnel*
CIRCONVALLAZIONE	*ring road*
RALLENTARE	*slow down*
SENSO UNICO	*one way street*

By train

There are four categories of train – **Locale** (very slow stopping train), **Diretto** (a bit quicker), **Espresso** (limited stop) and **Rapido** (express). There are also some special trains known as TEE (**Trans Europ Express**). If you take a **Rapido** or a TEE, you have to pay a supplement. You may also have to make a reservation in advance, as well as having to travel first class. You can check these details as well as train times in the timetable **l'orario**.

Milan and Rome both have an underground railway system **la metropolitana** or **il metro**.

Signs to look for

AI BINARI	*to the platforms*
BIGLIETTERIA	*ticket office*
GABINETTI/TOILETTE	*toilets*

And two words you might hear

RITARDO	*delay*
SCIOPERO	*strike*

By bus

In many large towns, automatic ticket machines have replaced conductors on the buses, and a one-price fare is in operation. In some places the ticket machines themselves have been superseded and you have to buy a ticket **un biglietto** at a **tabaccheria** before you get on the bus. Buses usually have the entry door **l'entrata** at the back and the exit **l'uscita** in the middle or at the front.

Police

There are three main kinds of police in Italy. **Vigili urbani** are town police mostly controlling traffic and are similar to traffic wardens, though they can give you a fine **una multa** on the spot or get your car towed away, so watch out for 'no parking' signs – **DIVIETO DI SOSTA** and **PERMANENTE CONTINUA**.

The **polizia** and the **carabinieri** are two separate forces, though their duties, in peace time, are similar. Both forces carry guns and administer on the spot fines.

To report a traffic accident, theft, etc, you can go either to the **carabinieri** or to the police station **la questura**.

Some more directions to listen for

al semaforo	*to/at the traffic lights*
all'incrocio	*to/at the cross-roads*
è lontano	*it's a long way*
è vicino	*it's close by*
è qui	*it's here*
è laggiù/è là in fondo	*it's down there*
dietro/davanti	*behind/in front*
di qua/là	*this/that way*

4 Getting somewhere to stay

Key words

Getting a room for two	**Ha una camera per due?**
I've got a reservation	**Ho una prenotazione**
What time's breakfast?	**A che ora è la colazione?**
A place at a campsite	**Ha un posto?**
Is the museum open today?	**E' aperto oggi il museo?**
20 30 40 . . .	**venti trenta quaranta . . .**

Conversations

At the reception desk

The hotel's full

Receptionist	Buona sera.
Tourist	Buona sera. Ha una camera?
Receptionist	No, mi dispiace, l'albergo è completo.

mi dispiace *I'm sorry*

Checking in when you have a reservation

Il signor Rossi	Buon giorno, ho una prenotazione.
Receptionist	Sì. Il Suo nome, per favore?
Il signor Rossi	Rossi.
Receptionist	Ah sì. E' il numero trecentoventicinque.

| Il signor Rossi | Trecentoventicinque. |
| Receptionist | Sì. Mi dia il passaporto, per favore. |

il Suo nome   *your name*
mi dia il passaporto   *would you give me your passport*

A room for two, for two nights, with bath

Tourist	Buona sera.
Receptionist	Buona sera.
Tourist	Ha una camera per due?
Receptionist	Per quanto tempo?
Tourist	Per due notti.
Receptionist	Sì, abbiamo una doppia con bagno. Va bene?
Tourist	Sì. Quant'è?
Receptionist	Venticinquemila lire con colazione.
Tourist	Bene.

What time is breakfast?

Tourist	A che ora è la colazione?
Receptionist	Dalle sette e mezzo alle nove e mezzo.
Tourist	Dalle sette e mezzo alle nove e mezzo. Bene.

dalle sette e mezzo alle nove e mezzo   *from 7.30 to 9.30*

At the campsite
A place for a tent, for two adults and two children

Tourist	Buona sera.
Receptionist	Buona sera.
Tourist	Ha un posto?
Receptionist	Sì. Per una tenda o una roulotte?
Tourist	Una tenda.
Receptionist	Per quante persone?
Tourist	Due adulti e due bambini.

una roulotte (*pronounced 'roo-**lot**'*)   *a caravan*

Getting information

Asking for a map of the town

Tourist	Ha una pianta della città, per favore?
Clerk	Sì, eccola.
Tourist	Grazie.
Clerk	Prego.

eccola *here it is*

Is the Etruscan Museum open today?

Tourist	E' aperto oggi il Museo Etrusco?
Clerk	No, il lunedì è chiuso, domani è aperto.

il lunedì è chiuso *it's closed on Mondays*

Explanations

Asking for accommodation

'Do you have a room?' is **ha una camera?**.

singola/doppia   *single/double*
con bagno/senza bagno *with bath/without bath*

To ask if someone has something, begin the question with **ha** and follow that with the word for what you want. The answer may well begin with **ho** (I have) or **abbiamo** (we have), eg **abbiamo una doppia**.

How long, how many?

You may be asked **per quanto tempo?** (for how long?), or **per quante persone?** (for how many people?).

per una notte/due notti *for one night/two nights*
per una persona/per due *for one person/for two*

When, what time?

To ask at what time something is happening, use **a che ora?**, eg **a che ora è la colazione?** (what time is breakfast?).

And to ask the time, you say **che ore sono?**.

You'll need to understand the times you hear

dalle sette e mezzo alle nove e mezzo	*from half-past seven to half-past nine*
le sette	*seven o'clock*
le sette e un quarto	*quarter past seven*
le sette e venti	*twenty past seven*
le sette e mezzo	*half-past seven*
le otto meno venti	*twenty to eight*
le otto meno un quarto	*quarter to eight*

Times of day

stamattina	*this morning*
stasera	*this evening*
oggi pomeriggio	*this afternoon*
dopo pranzo	*after lunch*

Is it open?

è aperto?	*is it open?*
è aperto domani?	*is it open tomorrow?*
è aperto oggi il museo?	*is the museum open today?*
è aperta stasera la discoteca?	*is the discothèque open this evening?*

More numbers

20	venti	60	sessanta
30	trenta	70	settanta
40	quaranta	80	ottanta
50	cinquanta	90	novanta

Exercises

1 Asking for things. Remember the pattern **ha una camera, per favore?**. Practise asking for the following things.
(NB: you don't need a word for 'some' after **ha**.)

a   a room with a bath for three nights
b   space for a caravan
c   some small change
d   two telephone tokens
e   a pen

2   Read these requests for accommodation out loud several times. Which arrangement best suits the people listed below?

a   una camera con tre letti e bagno per una settimana
b   una camera doppia e una singola
c   una singola con colazione per una notte
d   una doppia e una camera a due letti
e   una doppia con bagno per due settimane

i   Mr. and Mrs. Smith and their two daughters aged seven and nine
ii   Mr. and Mrs. Jones and their son aged seventeen
iii   Peter and Jane Scott spending a romantic honeymoon fortnight
iv   Mr. and Mrs. Robinson and their four-year-old daughter, staying a week
v   Bob Williams, student, just passing through

3   You're having a drink in the hotel bar and tell the barman to add it to the bill **(sul conto, per favore)**. He wants to know your room number. Say each number out loud in Italian, and then write it down.

a 204   b 510   c 115   d 317   e 412

4   You arrive at a campsite one evening. Complete this conversation.

You   (greet the lady at the desk) . . . .
. . . .

Receptionist	Buona sera. Mi dica.
You	*(you want space for a tent)* ....
	....
Receptionist	Per quanto tempo?
You	*(two or three nights)* ....
	....
Receptionist	Per quante persone?
You	*(two adults and three children)* ....
	....
Receptionist	Bene.
You	*(ask what time the supermarket is open)* ....
	....
Receptionist	Dalle sette e mezzo all'una, e dalle cinque alle nove e mezzo.
You	*(you need a plan of the town)* .....
	....
Receptionist	Eccola.
You	*(thank her and say goodbye)* ......
	....

5 Practise saying these times out loud – check your pronunciation with that at the end of Programme 4 on the cassette. Then work out what the times are and jot them down.

a le sei meno dieci
b l'una e venti
c le quattro meno un quarto
d le undici e un quarto
e le tre e mezzo

Worth knowing

Getting a hotel room

Information about hotels and pensions can be obtained from the Italian State Tourist Office in London or Dublin (see page 59 for addresses).

If you haven't booked in advance, you can get advice from a Provincial Tourist Board **Ente Provinciale Turismo** in any of the 95 provincial capitals, or from a Local Tourist Board **Azienda Autonoma di Soggiorno,** of which there are over 400 in tourist resorts. Sometimes these offices will even phone round to hotels for you.

If you want a double room you can ask for **una doppia,** though this won't guarantee a double bed **un letto matrimoniale.** A room with two beds is **una camera a due letti;** with three beds – **a tre letti,** etc. A room with a shower is **con doccia.**
Full board is **pensione completa;** half board is **mezza pensione.**

La colazione (breakfast), sometimes called **la prima colazione,** will usually consist of **brioches,** or **pane con burro e marmellata** (bread with butter and jam), washed down with **caffelatte.**

Hotels

Hotels **alberghi** are classified as De Luxe, First, Second, Third and Fourth class. **Pensioni,** offering more modest accommodation, are also First, Second or Third class. The bill **il conto** usually includes all service charges **servizio** and VAT (**l'IVA,** pronounced '**lee**-va'). Check by asking **il servizio è compreso?**. And one other important word is **la chiave** (the key).

Youth hostels

There are only 50 or so **alberghi** or **ostelli per la gioventù,** so it's as well to book – YHA members only. For addresses see page 59.

Camping

Campsites **campeggi** are plentiful and generally well-maintained. Discounts are available for

campers holding the International Camping Carnet
(get it from the AA or RAC).

A few useful words

la bombola	*gas-bottle*
il ghiaccio	*ice*
il rimorchio	*trailer*
la presa di corrente	*electric point*

Musei e gallerie d'arte Museums and art galleries

Italy has a wealth of museums, art galleries and
other tourist attractions – but note that most of
them are closed on Mondays.

More places to visit

il castello	*the castle*	la chiesa	*the church*
il mercato	*the market*	la piscina	*the swimming pool*
il palazzo	*the palace*	la spiaggia	*the beach*
il teatro	*the theatre*	la torre	*the tower*

5 A meal and a chat

Key words

Ordering three pizzas and a mixed salad	**Tre pizze e un'insalata mista**
And a litre of red wine	**E un litro di vino rosso**
Introducing people	**Le presento . . .Piacere**
How are you?	**Come sta?**
Very well!	**Benissimo!**
May I?	**Posso?**

Conversations

At the pizzeria

Getting a table for three

Waiter   Buona sera. Quanti sono?
Customer Tre.
Waiter   Porto il menù.

quanti sono? *how many are you?*
porto il menù *I'll bring the menu*

Ordering

Customer Tre pizze – una napoletana, una ai funghi e una quattro stagioni.
Waiter   Una napoletana, una ai funghi e una quattro stagioni. E' tutto?
Customer E un'insalata mista per tre.
Waiter   E da bere?
Customer Un litro di vino rosso e una mezza minerale.

ai funghi *with mushrooms*
è tutto? *is that all?*
e da bere? *and to drink?*
una mezza minerale *a half of mineral water*

Toilets?

Customer	La toilette, per favore?
Waiter	Laggiù a destra.

The bill, please

Waiter	Caffè?
Customer	No, grazie. Il conto, per favore.

Meeting people
Introductions

La signora Fabbri	Le presento il signor Rossi, il signor Jones – inglese.
Il signor Rossi	Piacere.
Il signor Jones	Piacere.

piacere *it's a pleasure*

How are you?

La signora Fabbri	Come sta?
Il signor Jones	Bene, grazie, e Lei?
La signora Fabbri	Benissimo.

e Lei? *and you?*

Do you like . . .?

Girl	Le piace Firenze?
Visitor	Sì, moltissimo.
Girl	E la cucina toscana?
Visitor	Sì, mi piace.

la cucina toscana *Tuscan cuisine*

The weather – it's hot today, isn't it?

Man	Fa molto caldo oggi, no?
Woman	Sì, molto caldo.

May I? Oops, sorry!

Man	Posso?
Woman	Prego.
Man	Oh, mi dispiace!

Explanations

Likes and dislikes

To ask if someone likes something, **le piace?**

le piace?	*do you like it?*
le piace l'Italia?	*do you like Italy?*
le piace la pizza?	*do you like the pizza?*

To say you like something, **mi piace**

mi piace (moltissimo)	*I like it (very much)*
mi piace l'Italia	*I like Italy*

and if you don't like it – **non mi piace.**

Meeting people

When you're introduced to someone, the word to use is **piacere** (it's a pleasure/delighted)

Asking how someone is – **come sta?** (how are you). The usual reply is **bene, grazie** (fine, thanks), or **benissimo** (very well – the ending **-issimo** is like 'very' in English). And to ask how the other person is, **e Lei?**

More politeness

posso?	*may I? (when you're borrowing someone's newspaper, cadging a light, etc)*
prego	*please do*
mi dispiace	*I'm sorry*
permesso?	*excuse me (when you want to get past someone)*

Describing things

In Italian, most descriptive words (adjectives) come after the words they describe

acqua minerale	*mineral water*
vino rosso, vino bianco	*red wine, white wine*
insalata mista	*mixed salad*
acqua calda	*hot water*

The last letter of the adjective usually alters, according to what it's referring to, ie it can be masculine or feminine, singular or plural

pizza napoletana *(f.sg.)*   pizze napoletane *(f.pl.)*
vino napoletano *(m.sg.)*   vini napoletani *(m.pl.)*

Four very useful adjectives

bello,-a	*lovely, pretty*
buono,-a	*good, nice*
grande	*big*
piccolo,-a	*small*

Grande, inglese, and other adjectives ending in **-e** do not change in the singular, and all end in **-i** in the plural.

Exercises

1   What do you say in these situations?

a   you want to find out when supper **la cena** is served
b   you're chatting to a waiter who's been to England and you want to ask if he likes English cooking
c   at supper you want to borrow the salt from someone else's table
d   you knock over a glass of wine
e   you're introduced to someone
f   you want to ask how someone is
g   you ask someone to direct you to the 'Barbarella' discothèque.

2   Complete these phrases from a waiter's order – pair each with a suitable word from the list below.

a   una pizza . . . .
b   un'acqua . . . .
c   un'insalata . . . .
d   mezzo litro di vino . . . .
e   un caffè . . . .

mista   napoletana   bianco   corretto   minerale

3 You and your family arrive at the **pizzeria**. Fill in the gaps in this dialogue.

Waiter	Buona sera. Quanti sono?
You	*(there are five of you)* ....
Waiter	Va bene questo tavolo?
You	*(yes, that's fine)* ....
Waiter	Bene. Porto il menù.

You study the menu and decide on five pizzas with mushrooms

Waiter	Desidera?
You	*(give him your order)* ....
	....
Waiter	E' tutto?
You	*(you'll have a mixed salad for five)*
	....
Waiter	E da bere?
You	*(you want a litre of red wine and a half of mineral water)* ....
	....

When you've finished eating, the waiter returns

Waiter	Caffè?
You	*(two coffees, one of them laced with brandy)* ....
	....
Waiter	Nient'altro?
You	*(no, thanks – the bill, please)* ......
	....
Waiter	Ecco.
You	*(ask if service is included)* ....
	....
Waiter	Sì.
You	*(thank him and say goodbye)* .....
	....

4 Practise your pronunciation – check it with the end of Programme 5 on the cassette.

a   Fa molto caldo oggi, no?
b   Le piace l'Inghilterra?
c   Che ore sono?
d   Come sta?
e   Ha spiccioli, per favore?

Worth knowing

Where to eat

For a light meal or a snack, look out for **una pizzeria, una rosticceria** or **una tavola calda**. For a full meal, **un ristorante** is usually more expensive than **una trattoria**.

Menus

Il menù turistico is the fixed-price meal, providing a limited choice of dishes.

Menus are usually divided into various sections

antipasti	*hors d'oeuvres*
minestre *or* primi	*first courses, including pasta*
pietanze *or* secondi piatti	*main courses*
contorni	*vegetables*
dolci	*desserts*

You'll usually find there's a cover charge **pane e coperto** which includes the cost of bread. Service is usually included.

Common dishes

cotoletta alla milanese	*veal cutlet in breadcrumbs*
frutti di mare	*mixed sea food*
ossobuco	*knuckle of veal in tomato sauce, served with rice*
pollo alla cacciatora	*chicken in red wine*
saltimbocca alla romana	*veal escalopes with ham and sage*

Pasta

Pasta comes in many different shapes and sizes, with a variety of tasty sauces, eg

salsa bolognese *or* ragù
meat, tomato and parmesan

pesto
fresh basil, garlic, pine nuts and pecorino cheese

alla carbonara
eggs, bacon and pecorino

Pizza

As pizzas have travelled so well, you'll probably know some of these common types

pizza napoletana	*basic pizza with tomatoes, mozzarella cheese and anchovies*
pizza margherita	*tomatoes, mozzarella and oregano*
pizza ai funghi	*with mushrooms*
pizza quattro stagioni	*literally 'four seasons', four varieties in one*
pizza capricciosa	*literally at the whim of the chef, but usually with tomatoes, artichokes, capers, anchovies, olives and mozzarella*

Wines

Among the best known white wines **vini bianchi** are **Frascati** from Rome, **Orvieto** from Umbria, **Asti Spumante** sweet sparkling wine from Piedmont, **Soave** from Veneto, and **Tokai** from Friuli. Red wines **vini rossi** include **Barolo** and **Barbera** from Piedmont, **Bardolino** and **Valpolicella** from Veneto, and **Chianti** from Tuscany.

Can you 'GET BY'?

Test

Try these exercises when you've finished the course – the answers are on page 62.

1   Match each question with the place where it might be asked – choose from the list below.

a   E una bistecca, va bene così?
b   Ecco le borsette, quale le piace?
c   Nient'altro, un po' di formaggio?
d   Per cartoline o lettere?
e   Con doccia o con bagno?
f   E da bere?
g   Andata e ritorno?
h   Per una tenda o una roulotte?

all'albergo   al ristorante   alla macelleria
alla stazione   alla pelletteria   alla posta
al campeggio   al ristorante

2   Choose the correct alternatives.
a   You've got a sweet tooth. Which of these would you put in your tea?
   lo zucchero   gli spiccioli   un bicchiere

b   Which of these would you stick on your **cartolina?**
   uno sciopero   un francobollo   un fiammifero

c   You want five telephone tokens. Which do you ask for?
   cinque etti di prosciutto   cinque portafogli
   cinque gettoni

d   Which of these might you buy by the **etto?**
   formaggio   latte   benzina

e You've got a reservation. You say **ho una** . . .
   colazione prenotazione stazione

f You're leaving tomorrow – that's
   domani oggi lunedì

3 Ask for the following items.

a an orangeade and a beer
b a litre of white wine and a mineral water
c two pizzas with mushrooms and a mixed salad
d a bit of cured ham
e spaghetti with a sauce of eggs, bacon and
   cheese

4 Questions, questions! Find the most likely
answer to each one.

a La toilette, per favore?
b E' aperto oggi il ristorante?
c Fa molto caldo, no?
d Dove abita in Italia?
e Come sta?
f Le piace così?

i Trieste. ii Benissimo, grazie. iii Sì, molto.
iv Oggi, no – domani, sì. v Là in fondo.
vi No, così no.

5 What might you reply when someone says . . .

a Le piace la spiaggia? (and you do, very much)
b Va bene così? (and you've been given too
   much)
c Posso? (and you don't mind her smoking)
d Gorgonzola o Bel Paese? (and you're not sure
   which is which)
e Le presento la signorina Ferrari. (and it's a
   pleasure)
f Ha bisogno di altro? (and you don't want
   anything else)
g Come sta? (and you're feeling fine)
h Un tè? (and you want to say 'yes, please')

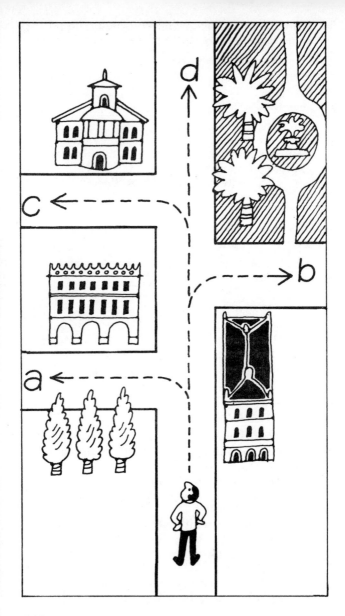

6   Using the map opposite, how would you tell someone to follow the route of the arrows in each case?

a   prenda ....

    ....

b   prenda ....

    ....

c   prenda ....

    ....

d   ....

7   Which sign would you look for if you wanted . . .

a   a bus stop
b   the ring road
c   the city centre
d   the underground railway in Rome
e   a motorway
f   a police station

QUESTURA   AUTOSTRADA   CENTRO CITTA'   FERMATA
DIVIETO DI SOSTA   CIRCONVALLAZIONE   METROPOLITANA

And there's a sign left over – what does it mean?

8   What could you say if . . .

a   you meet someone at 6 pm
b   you're enquiring about the price
c   you decide to buy this one
d   you're making your way through a crowd
e   you're sorry you've bumped into someone
f   you don't understand
g   you want to know when it's open

Reference section

Pronunciation

When you're practising Italian words and phrases, concentrate on clear pronunciation and on the sing-song intonation of the language (it's worth exaggerating to start with).

There's no substitute of course for listening to native Italian speakers and copying them, but the following brief guide will be useful when you're reading through the conversations. It gives approximate English equivalents of Italian sounds.

Vowels Italian vowels are similar to English vowels, but they are 'purer' sounds and you need to open your mouth wider to say them clearly.

Be especially careful with

a	like 'a' in 'what'	alla casa
e	like 'ai' in 'pair'	per favore
i	like 'ee' in 'sweet'	pizza ai funghi
u	like 'oo' in 'boot'	numero due

Consonants Most sound similar to English, but pay special attention to the following combinations

ci	like 'ch' in 'chess'	ciao
gi	like 'j' in 'John'	buon giorno
ch	like 'k' in 'kilo'	chilo
gh	like 'g' in 'get'	alberghi
gli	like 'lli' in 'billiards'	biglietto
gn	like 'ny' in 'canyon'	bagno
qu	like 'qu' in 'request'	questo
sc	like 'sh' in 'shop'	pesce
z	like 'ts' in 'cats'	zucchero, colazione
	or like 'dz'	zero, mezzo

h is always silent

a single **s** between vowels
is usually like 's' in 'rose'   de**s**idera

Double consonants should be lingered over, to distinguish them from single consonants.

Stress Usually stress is placed on the last but one syllable

pro**sciut**to   passa**por**to

A few words have an irregular stress, ie not on this last but one syllable

lettera   **gra**zie

If a word ends with an accent, stress the accented syllable

cit**tà**   caf**fè**

Some of the words with irregular stress that you meet in the chapters of **Getting by in Italian** are listed below, with their chapter number.

1 **gra**zie **es**tera s'ac**co**modi **ta**volo **zuc**chero **sem**plice
2 **fra**gola de**si**dera **let**tere te**le**foni **spic**cioli fiam**mi**feri fruttiven**do**lo
3 **au**tobus bi**na**rio **nu**mero re**pub**blica **ra**pido **scio**pero se**ma**foro **un**dici, **do**dici, etc
4 **ca**mera **dop**pia **sin**gola ser**vi**zio **bom**bola
5 be**nis**simo mol**tis**simo I**ta**lia **pic**colo tu**ris**tico

---

Extra language notes

'A' and 'the'

There are several words for 'a' and 'the'

un/il francobollo	with masculine words
una/la lettera	with feminine words
un/l'albergo (m.)	before words beginning
un'/l'aranciata (f.)	with a vowel
uno/lo scontrino	before a masculine word beginning with **z**, or **s** plus a consonant, eg **sc, sp**

With plural words, 'the' can be

i francobolli	with masculine words
le lettere	with feminine words
gli spaghetti	before words beginning
gli alberghi	with **z**, a vowel or **s**
	plus a consonant,
	eg **sc, sp**

To say 'to the' or 'at the', you combine **a** with **il** or **la** to give **al** **duomo**, **alla** **piazza**.

Asking questions

You can ask questions by raising the pitch of your voice at the end of a sentence, eg in Programme 5
e la cucina italiana, le piace?

You can also add **vero?** or just **no?** at the end to give the meaning 'isn't it?'
fa molto caldo, no?

There are also a number of question words

che cosa?	*what?*	perché?	*why?*
chi?	*who?*	quando?	*when?*
come?	*what?/how?*	quanto,-a?	*how much?*
dove?	*where?*	quanti,-e?	*how many?*

Asking what things are

come si chiama?	*what's it called?*
cos'è questo?	*what's this?*
cosa sono questi?	*what are these?*
come si dice	*how do you say it*
in inglese?	*in English?*
in italiano?	*in Italian?*

Verbs

Although you can 'get by' without learning lists of verbs, some useful words taken from three common verbs are

going	**vado**	I'm going
	va	he's going, etc
	andiamo	we're going, let's go
	vanno	they're going

being	**sono**	I'm
	è	he's, she's, it's; you're
	siamo	we're
	sono	they're
	c'è	there is
	ci sono	there are
having	**ho**	I've
	ha	he has, etc
	abbiamo	we've
	hanno	they've

You can use this verb to say that you're

in pain	ho male
hot, cold	ho caldo, ho freddo
hungry, thirsty	ho fame, ho sete
needing a doctor	ho bisogno di un medico

'Can I . . .?' – start with **posso**, then follow it with any verb from the dictionary, eg

can I see?	posso vedere?
can I try it (on)?	posso provare?
can I telephone?	posso telefonare?

To get across the idea of 'not' and make the verb negative, just put **non** in front of it

| non capisco | *I don't understand* |

Numbers

0	**zero**	9	**nove**	18	**diciotto**
1	**uno**	10	**dieci**	19	**diciannove**
2	**due**	11	**undici**	20	**venti**
3	**tre**	12	**dodici**	21	**ventuno**
4	**quattro**	13	**tredici**	22	**ventidue**
5	**cinque**	14	**quattordici**	23	**ventitré**
6	**sei**	15	**quindici**	24	**ventiquattro** etc
7	**sette**	16	**sedici**	30	**trenta**
8	**otto**	17	**diciassette**	40	**quaranta**

50	cinquanta	1000	mille
60	sessanta	2000	duemila
70	settanta	3000	tremila *etc*
80	ottanta	1.000.000	un milione
90	novanta	2.000.000	due milioni
100	cento	1.000.000.000	un miliardo
150	cento-cinquanta	2.000.000.000	due miliardi
200	duecento		
300	trecento *etc*	1981	millenovecentottantuno

Days of the week

lunedì	*Monday*	venerdì	*Friday*
martedì	*Tuesday*	sabato	*Saturday*
mercoledì	*Wednesday*	domenica	*Sunday*
giovedì	*Thursday*		

Months of the year

gennaio	*January*	luglio	*July*
febbraio	*February*	agosto	*August*
marzo	*March*	settembre	*September*
aprile	*April*	ottobre	*October*
maggio	*May*	novembre	*November*
giugno	*June*	dicembre	*December*

The Four Seasons

Spring	**la primavera**	*lah pree-mah-vEH-rah*
Summer	**l'estate**	*leh-stAH-teh*
Fall	**l'autunno**	*lah-oo-tOOn-noh*
Winter	**l'inverno**	*leen-vEHr-noh*

The Weather

How is the weather today?	**Che tempo fa oggi?** *kay tEHm-poh fAH OH-jee*
It's good (bad) weather.	**Fa bel (cattivo) tempo.** *fah behl (kaht-tEE-voh) tEHm-poh*
It's hot.	**Fa caldo.** *fah kAHl-doh*
cold	**freddo** *frAYd-doh*
cool	**fresco** *frAY-skoh*
It's windy.	**Tira vento.** *tEE-rah vEHn-toh*
It's sunny.	**C'è il sole.** *chEH eel sOH-leh*
It's raining.	**Piove.** *pee-OH-veh*
It's snowing.	**Nevica.** *nAY-vee-kah*
It's drizzling.	**Pioviggina.** *pee-oh-vEE-jee-nah*

Temperature Conversions

To change Fahrenheit to Centigrade, subtract 32 and multiply by $\frac{5}{9}$.

To change Centigrade to Fahrenheit, multiply by $\frac{9}{5}$ and add 32.

Gradi

Centigradi   Fahrenheit

Termòmetro

Weights and Measures

Centimeters / Inches

It is usually unnecessary to make exact conversions from your customary inches to the metric system used in Italy, but to give you an approximate idea of how they compare, we give you the following guide.

To convert **centimetri** into inches, multiply by .39.
To convert inches into **centimetri,** multiply by 2.54.

Centimetri

Pollici

Meters / Feet

1 meter (metro) = 39.37 inches
                = 3.28 feet
                = 1.09 yards

1 foot = 0.3 meters
1 yard = 0.9 meters

Kilograms / Pounds

1 kilogram **(chilo)** = 2.2 pounds
1 pound   = 0.45 kilogram

Liters / Quarts

1 liter = 1.06 quarts
4 liters = 1.06 gallons

For quick approximate conversion, multiply the number of gallons by 4 to get liters **(litri).** Divide the number of liters by 4 to get gallons.

CLOTHING MEASUREMENTS

WOMEN

Shoes

American	4	5	6	7	8	9
British	3	4	5	6	7	8
Continental	35	36	37	38	39	40

Dresses, suits

American	8	10	12	14	16	18
British	10	12	14	16	18	20
Continental	36	38	40	42	44	46

Blouses, sweaters

American	32	34	36	38	40	42
British	34	36	38	40	42	44
Continental	40	42	44	46	48	50

MEN

Shoes

American	7	8	9	10	11	12
British	6	7	8	9	10	11
Continental	39	41	43	44	45	46

Suits, coats

American	34	36	38	40	42	44	46	48
British	44	46	48	50	54	56	58	60
Continental	44	46	48	50	52	54	56	58

Shirts

American	14	$14\frac{1}{2}$	15	$15\frac{1}{2}$	16	$16\frac{1}{2}$	17	$17\frac{1}{2}$
British	14	$14\frac{1}{2}$	15	$15\frac{1}{2}$	16	$16\frac{1}{2}$	17	$17\frac{1}{2}$
Continental	36	37	38	39	40	41	42	43

Exchanging Money

Where is the currency exchange (bank)?	**Dov'è l'ufficio di cambio (la banca)?** *doh-vEH loof-fEE-chee-oh dee kAHm-bee-oh (lah bAHn-kah)*
I wish to change ____.	**Desidero cambiare ____.** *day sEE-deh-roh kahm-bee-AH-reh*
money	**il denaro** *eel deh-nAH-roh*
dollars (pounds)	**i dollari (le sterline)** *ee-dOHl-lah-ree (le stehr-lEE-neh)*
traveler's checks	**traveler's checks (assegni da viaggiatori)** *(ahs-sEH-ny dah vee-ah jee-ah tOH-ree)*
May I cash a personal check?	**Posso cambiare un assegno personale?** *pOHs-soh kahm-bee-AH-reh oon ahs-sEH-ny-ee-oh pehr-soh-nAH-leh*
What's the current exchange rate for dollars (pounds)?	**Qual è il cambio corrente del dollaro (della sterlina)?** *koo-ahl-EH eel kAHm-bee-oh kohr-rEHn-teh dayl dOHl-lah-roh (dAYl-lah stehr-lEE-nah)*
What commission do you charge?	**Quale percentuale vi fate pagare?** *koo-AH-leh pehr-chehn-too-AH-leh vee fAH-teh pah-gAH-reh*
Where do I sign?	**Dove debbo firmare?** *dOH-veh dAYb-boh feer-mAH-reh*
I'd like the money ____.	**Vorrei i soldi ____.** *vohr-rEH-ee ee sOHl-dee*
in large (small) bills	**in grosse (piccole) banconote** *een grOHs-seh (pEEk-oh-leh) bahn-koh-nOH-teh*
in small change	**in spiccioli** *een spee-chee-oh-lee*

Important Signs

Acqua (non)potabile	(Not) potable water
Alt	Stop
Aperto	Open
Attenzione	Caution, watch out
Avanti	Enter (come in, go, walk [at the lights])
Caldo or "C"	Hot
Chiuso	Closed
Divieto di sosta	No parking
Divieto di transito	No entrance, keep out
Freddo or "F"	Cold
Gabinetti (WC)	Toilets
Ingresso	Entrance
Libero	Vacant
Non toccare	Hands off, don't touch
Occupato	Occupied
Pericolo	Danger
Riservato	Reserved
Si vende	For sale
Signora	Women's room
Signore	Men's room
Spingere	Push
Tirare	Pull
Uscita	Exit
Vietato fumare	No smoking

Guarded railroad crossing

Yield

Stop

Right of way

Dangerous intersection ahead

Gasoline (petrol) ahead

Parking

No vehicles allowed

Dangerous curve

Pedestrian crossing

Oncoming traffic has right of way

No bicycles allowed

No parking allowed

No entry

No left turn

No U-turn

No passing

Border crossing

Traffic signal ahead

Speed limit

Traffic circle (roundabout) ahead

Minimum speed limit

All traffic turns left

End of no passing zone

One-way street

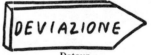
Detour

Danger ahead

Entrance to expressway

Expressway ends

Menu Items

Appetizers (Starters)

Antipasti mostly consist of raw salads, cooked chilled vegetables dressed with a vinaigrette, and massive varieties of sausages and salamis. Some key terms are:

acciughe	*ah-chee-OH-gheh*	anchovies
antipasto misto	*ahn-tee-pAHs-toh mEEs-toh*	assorted appetizers
carciofi	*kahr-chee-OH-fee*	artichoke
mortadella	*mohr-tah-dEHl-lah*	cold sausage, similar to bologna
prosciutto crudo	*proh-shee-OOt-toh krOO-doh*	raw cured ham
tartufi	*tahr-tOO-fee*	truffles (white)

Soups

Soups can be either thick or thin, and thus are given different names. **Brodi** are generally broths, while **zuppe** are thick and hearty.

brodo di manzo	*brOH-doh dee mAHn-tsoh*	broth, generally meat-based
brodo di pollo	*brOH-hod dee pOHl-loh*	chicken broth
brodo magro di vegetali	*brOH-doh mAH-groh dee veh-jeh-tAH-lee*	vegetable broth
crema di ___	*krEH-mah dee*	creamed ___ soup
cacciucco	*kah-chee-OO-koh*	seafood chowder
minestra in brodo	*mee-nEHs-trah een brOH-doh*	pasta in broth
minestrone	*mee-nehs-trOH-neh*	thick vegetable soup
zuppa di ___	*tsOOp-pah dee*	thick soup

Entrees (Meat and Fish Dishes)

The "main course" of an Italian meal is usually somewhat plain, either a sautéed or grilled meat or a baked fish or chicken. Along the coast and in Sicily and Sardinia, you'll find unusual and exciting varieties of seafood.

acciughe	*ah-chee-OO-gheh*	anchovies
anguille	*ahn-goo-EEl-leh*	eel
aragosta	*ah-rah-gOHs-tah*	lobster (spiny)
aringa	*ah-rEEn-gah*	herring
affumicata	*ahf-foo-mee-kAH-tah*	smoked
baccalà	*bah-kah-lAH*	dried salt cod
branzino (nasello)	*brahn-tsEE-noh (nah-sEHl-loh)*	bass (hake)
calamari (seppie)	*kah-lah-mAH-ree (sAYp-pee-eh)*	squid
cozze	*kOH-tseh*	mussels
gamberetti	*gAHm-beh-rAY-tee*	prawns
granchi	*grAHn-key*	crabs
lumache	*loo-mAH-keh*	snails
merluzzo	*mayr-lOOt-tsoh*	cod
ostriche	*OHs-tree-keh*	oysters
polipo	*pOH-lee-poh*	octopus
salmone	*sahl-mOH-neh*	salmon
sardine	*sahr-dEE-neh*	sardines
scampi	*skAHm-pee*	shrimps
sogliola	*sOH-ly-ee-oh-lah*	flounder (sole)
trota	*trOH-tah*	trout
tonno	*tOHn-noh*	tuna

vongole	vOHn-goh-leh	clams
trance di pesce alla griglia	trAHn-cheh dee pAY-sheh AHl-lah grEE-ly-ee-ah	grilled fish steaks
fritto misto di pesce	frEEt-toh mEEs-toh dee pAY-sheh	mised fried fish

Meat dishes are often sauced or served with some type of gravy. Here are some basic terms you'll encounter on Italian menus.

agnello (abbacchio)	ah-ny-EHl-loh (ahb-bAH-key-oh)	lamb
capretto	kah-prAYy-toh)	goat
maiale	mah-ee-AH-leh	pork
manzo	mAHn-tsoh	beef
montone	mohn-tOH-neh	mutton
vitello	vee-tEHl-loh	veal

And some common cuts of meat, plus other terms you'll find on a menu:

affettati	ahf-fayt-tAH-tee	cold cuts
costate	kohs-tAH-teh	chops
animelle	ah-nee-mEHl-leh	sweetbreads
cervello	chehr-vEHl-loh	brains
fegato	fAY-gah-toh	liver
bistecca	bees-tAY-kah	steak
lingua	lEEn-goo-ah	tongue
pancetta	pahn-chAYt-tah	bacon
polpette	pohl-pAYt-teh	meatballs
prosciutto cotto	proh-shee-OOt-toh kOHt-toh	ham (cooked)

rognoni	*roh-ny-OH-nee*	kidneys

And some terms for fowl and game:

anitra	*AH-nee-trah*	duck
beccaccia	*bay-kAH-chee-ah*	woodcock
cappone	*kahp-pOH-neh*	capon
carne di cervo	*kAHr-neh dee chEHr-voh*	venison
coniglio	*koh-nEE-ly-ee-oh*	rabbit
fagiano	*fah-jee-AH-noh*	pheasant
faraona	*fah-rah-OH-nah*	guinea fowl
lepre	*lEH-preh*	hare
oca	*OH-kah*	goose
pernice	*pehr-nEE-cheh*	partridge
piccioncino	*pEE-chee-ohn-chEE-noh*	squab (pigeon)
pollo	*pOHl-loh*	chicken
porcellino di latte	*pohr-chehl-lEE-noh dee lAHz-teh*	suckling pig
quaglia	*koo-AH-ly-ee-ah*	quail
tacchino	*tah-kEY-noh*	turkey

Vegetables

asparagi	*ahs-pAH-rah-jee*	asparagus
carciofi	*kahr-chee-OH-fee*	artichoke
carote	*kah-rOH-teh*	carrots
cavoli	*kAH-voh-lee*	cabbage
cavolfiori	*kah-vohl-fee-OH-ree*	cauliflower
cetriolo	*cheh-tree-OO-loh*	cucumber

ceci	*chay-chee*	chick-peas
fagioli	*fah-jee-oh-IEE*	beans (dried)
fagiolini	*fah-jee-oh-IEE-nee*	green beans
fave	*fAH-veh*	broad beans
funghi	*fOOn-ghee*	mushrooms
lattuga	*laht-tOO-gah*	lettuce
lenticchie	*len-tEE-key-eh*	lentils
granturco	*grahn-tOO-rkoh*	corn (maize)
melanzana	*meh-lAHn-tsah-nah*	eggplant (aubergine)
peperoni	*peh-peh-rOH-nee*	pepper
patate	*pah-tAH-teh*	potatoes
patatine fritte	*pah-tah-tEE-neh frEEt-teh*	French fries (chips)
piselli	*pee-sEHl-lee*	peas
pomodoro	*poh-moh-dOH-roh*	tomato
porcini	*pohr-chee-nee*	wild mushroom
sedano	*sAY-dah-noh*	celery
spinaci	*spee-nAH-chee*	spinach

Cheese

There are many, many varieties of Italian cheeses. A few useful words you can use in discussing your choices:

Is the cheese ____ ?	**È il formaggio ____ ?**	*eh eel fohr-mAH-jee-oh*
mild	**dolce**	*dOHl-cheh*
sharp	**piccante**	*pee-kAHn-teh*
hard	**duro**	*dOO-roh*
soft	**molle**	*mOHl-leh*

Fruits

albicocca	*ahl-bee-kOH-kah*	apricot
ananasso	*ah-nah-nAHs-soh*	pineapple
anguria	*ahn-gOO-ree-ah*	watermelon
arancia	*ah-rAHn-chee-ah*	orange
castagne	*kahs-tAH-ny-eh*	chestnuts
cedro	*chAY-droh*	lime
ciliege	*chee-lee-EH-jee-eh*	cherries
datteri	*dAHt-teh-ree*	dates
fichi	*fEE-key*	figs
fragole	*frAH-goh-leh*	strawberries
lampone	*lahm-pOH-neh*	raspberry
limone	*lee-mOH-neh*	lemon
mandarini	*mahn-dah-rEE-nee*	tangerines
mandorle	*mAHn-dohr-leh*	almonds
mela	*mAY-lah*	apple
more	*mOH-reh*	mulberries
noci	*nOH-chee*	nuts
nocciole	*noh-chee-OH-leh*	hazelnuts (filberts)
melone	*meh-lOH-neh*	melon
pera	*pAY-rah*	pear
pesca	*pAYs-kah*	peach
pompelmo	*pohm-pEHl-moh*	grapefruit
prugne	*prOO-ny-eh*	plum
uva	*OO-vah*	grape

Geography

Countries and nationalities

l'America	USA	americano,-a	American
la Francia	France	francese	French
il Galles	Wales	gallese	Welsh
la Germania	Germany	tedesco,-a	German
l'Inghilterra	England	inglese	English
l'Irlanda	Ireland	irlandese	Irish
l'Italia	Italy	italiano,-a	Italian
la Scozia	Scotland	scozzese	Scottish

Cities and towns

Dublino	Dublin	Londra	London
Edimburgo	Edinburgh	Nuova York	New York
Firenze	Florence	Padova	Padua
Genova	Genoa	Roma	Rome
Livorno	Leghorn	Siracusa	Syracuse
Mantova	Mantua	Torino	Turin
Milano	Milan	Venezia	Venice
Napoli	Naples		

Useful addresses for Americans

Italian Government Travel Office (ENIT)
630 Fifth Avenue
New York, NY 10022
Tel: (212) 245-4825

Italian Government Travel Office (ENIT)
230 Michigan Avenue, North
Chicago, IL 60601
Tel: (312) DE2-1083

Consulate General of Italy
690 Park Avenue (at 69th Street)
New York, NY 10021
Tel: (212) 737-9100

ENIT publishes annually a free *Travellers Handbook* with information on the regions, holidays, travel, culture and leisure pursuits. The Handbook contains the addresses of all 52 **Alberghi per la Gioventù** (Youth Hostels).

ENIT also publishes an annual official list of all Italian hotels and pensions (**Annuario Alberghi**).

Key to exercises

Chapter 1

1   a   Due, per favore. Mille (1000) lire.
     b   Cinque, per favore. Duemilacinquecento (2500) lire.
     c   Quattro, per favore. Duemila (2000) lire.
     d   Tre, per favore. Millecinquecento (1500) lire.

2   Ciao, Gino.
     Un caffè e un cappuccino, per favore.
     E una pasta.
     Quant'è?
     Ecco duemila lire. Grazie.

3   a – iii   b – ii   c – i

5   a   Un caffè corretto, per favore. Quant'è?
     b   Un tè, una birra nazionale e una cioccolata calda. Quant'è?
     c   Un'aranciata e una spremuta di pompelmo. Quant'è?
     d   Una birra estera, un toast e un panino. Quant'è?
     e   Un cappuccino e un'acqua minerale. Quant'è?

Chapter 2

1   Cinque gelati, per favore.
     Quattro misti, e questo.
     (Da) cinquecento.
     (Ecco) duemilacinquecento lire.

2   due etti di prosciutto cotto
     mezzo litro di latte
     una bottiglia d'acqua minerale
     sei panini
     un etto di gorgonzola
     mezzo chilo di pomodori

un chilo di pesche
una bottiglia di birra

3 a un alimentari – prosciutto *(ham)*
  b un bar – un tè *(a tea)*
  c una tabaccheria – francobolli *(stamps)*
  d una gelateria – un gelato *(an ice-cream)*

4 a cinque cartoline
  b un francobollo per una cartolina
  c due francobolli per cartoline per l'Inghilterra
  d sigarette e fiammiferi
  e un cappuccino *(or* un caffelatte)

Chapter 3

1 Scusi, la biglietteria, per favore?
  Come? (Non capisco.)
  A sinistra – grazie.
  Due per Pisa, per favore.
  No, andata.
  Seconda classe, per favore.
  Your change would be seimila lire *(6000 lire).*

2 a il campeggio *(the campsite)* b la stazione *(the station)* c il duomo *(the cathedral)*
  d sinistra e destra f dritto

3 a CENTRO CITTA' b GABINETTI c IL DUOMO
  d USCITA e AI BINARI

4 a 11,650 lire *(football, Internazionale v. Fiorentina)*
  b 18,400 lire *(train, Rome—Trieste)*
  c 150 lire *(underground)*
  d 500 lire *(zoo)*
  e 15,850 lire *(beach — 6 cabins and beach umbrella)*

Chapter 4

1 a Ha una camera con bagno per tre notti, per favore?
  b Ha un posto per una roulotte, per favore?
  c Ha spiccioli, per favore?
  d Ha due gettoni, per favore?
  e Ha una penna, per favore?

2 a – iv b – ii c – v d – i e – iii

3 a duecentoquattro b cinquecentodieci c centoquindici
  d trecentodiciassette e quattrocentododici

4 Buona sera (signora).
  Ha un posto per una tenda, per favore?
  Due o tre notti.
  Due adulti e tre bambini.
  A che ora è aperto il supermercato?

Ha una pianta della città, per favore?
Grazie, arrivederci.

5 a ten to six b twenty past one c quarter to four
   d quarter past eleven e half-past three

Chapter 5

1 a A che ora è la cena? b Le piace la cucina inglese?
   c Posso? d Oh, mi dispiace! e Piacere. f Come sta?
   g Scusi, la discoteca 'Barbarella', per favore?

2 a una pizza napoletana b un'acqua minerale
   c un'insalata mista d mezzo litro di vino bianco
   e un caffè corretto

3 Cinque.
   Sì, va bene.
   Cinque pizze ai funghi, per favore.
   E un'insalata mista per cinque.
   Un litro di vino rosso e una mezza minerale.
   Un caffè e un caffè corretto, per favore.
   No, grazie – il conto, per favore.
   Il servizio è compreso?
   Grazie, arrivederci.

Test

1 a alla macelleria b alla pelletteria c al ristorante
   d alla posta e all'albergo f al ristorante g alla stazione
   h al campeggio

2 a lo zucchero b un francobollo c cinque gettoni
   d formaggio e prenotazione f domani

3 a un'aranciata e una birra
   b un litro di vino bianco e un'acqua minerale
   c due pizze ai funghi e un'insalata mista
   d un po' di prosciutto crudo e spaghetti alla carbonara

4 a – v b – iv c – iii d – i e – ii f – vi

5 a Sì, (mi piace) moltissimo. b No, è troppo. c Prego.
   d Questo. e Piacere. f No, grazie.
   g Bene/Benissimo, grazie (e Lei?). h Sì, grazie.

6 a . . . la prima (strada) a sinistra b . . . la prima (strada)
   a destra c . . . la seconda (strada) a sinistra
   d dritto (sempre dritto)

7 a FERMATA b CIRCONVALLAZIONE c CENTRO CITTA'
   d METROPOLITANA e AUTOSTRADA f QUESTURA
   The sign left over is DIVIETO DI SOSTA – *no parking*

8 a Buona sera. b Quant'è? c Prendo questo.
   d Permesso? e Oh, mi dispiace! f Non capisco.
   g A che ora è aperto?

Italian–English word list

NB: All translations given are as used in this book.

Bold type shows where the stress falls in each word.

Abbreviations: *m.* = masculine, *f.* = feminine, *sg.* = singular, *pl.* = plural.

Words given in the form *aperto,-a* have different endings for masculine and feminine (see page 46).

A

a *at, to*
ab**bia**mo *we have*
abita: **do**ve **abi**ta? *where do you live?*
ac**cen**dere *to switch on*
ac**co**modi: s'ac**co**modi *sit down; please go*
l' **ac**qua *(f.) water;*
l' **ac**qua mine**ra**le *mineral water;*
l' **ac**qua **sem**plice *ordinary water*
l' a**dul**to *adult*
ai (=a+i) *to the;*
  ai **fun**ghi *with mushrooms*
ai**u**to! *help!*
al (=a+il) *at/to the;*
al **lat**te/li**mo**ne *with milk/lemon*
l' al**ber**go *(m.; pl. al**ber**ghi) hotel*
l' alimen**ta**ri *(m.) grocer's*
all' = a+l'
alla (=a+la) *at/to the; flavour, style, eg*
alla **fra**gola *strawberry flavour;*
alla mila**ne**se *Milan style*
alle (=a+le) *(+time) until . . .*
al**lo**ra *then*
altri,-e *others*
altro *anything else;*
nient'**al**tro? *anything else?*

l' amba**scia**ta *(f.) embassy*
l' ambu**lan**za *(f.) ambulance*
an**da**ta *single;*
an**da**ta e ri**tor**no *return*
an**dia**mo *we're going, let's go*
l' annu**a**rio *(m.) annual list*
l' anti**pas**to *(m.) hors d'oeuvres*
a**per**to,-a *open*
l' a**ran**cia *(f.) orange*
l' aran**cia**ta *(f.) orangeade*
arrive**der**ci *goodbye*
a**scol**ti! *listen!*
l' as**se**gno *(m.) cheque;*
la **car**ta as**se**gni *cheque card*
atten**zio**ne! *look out!*
l' **au**tobus *(m.) bus*
l' auto**stra**da *(f.) motorway*
a**zien**da: l'A**zien**da Au**to**noma di Sog**gior**no *Local Tourist Board*

B

il **ba**gno *bath*
il bam**bi**no *child*
la **ban**ca *bank*
la banco**no**ta *banknote*
il bar *bar*
il Bel Pa**e**se *mild, creamy cheese*

bello,-a *lovely, pretty*
bene *OK, fine;*
  va bene (così) *that's OK, fine (like that)*
benissimo *very well*
la benzina *petrol*
bere *to drink*
bianco,-a *(pl.* bianchi,-e*) white*
il bicchiere *glass*
la biglietteria *ticket office*
il biglietto *ticket*
il binario *platform*
la birra *beer*
bisogno: ha bisogno di? *do you need?;*
  ho bisogno di *I need*
la bistecca *steak*
bolognese *of Bologna*
la bombola *gas-bottle*
la borsa *bag*
la borsetta *handbag*
la bottiglia *bottle*
la brioche *(pronounced 'bree-osh') bun*
britannico,-a *British*
buono,-a *good, nice;*
  buon giorno *good day/morning;*
  buon viaggio *bon voyage, have a good trip;*
  buona notte *goodnight;*
  buona sera *good evening*
il burro *butter*

C

la cabina *bathing hut*
cacciatora: alla cacciatora *hunter's style – cooked with tomatoes, onions and wine*
il caffè *coffee; small black espresso coffee*
il caffelatte *white coffee*
caldo: fa caldo *it's hot;*
  ho caldo *I'm hot;*
caldo,-a *hot;*

la tavola calda *snack-bar;*
cambiare *to change*
il cambio *exchange*
la camera *room*
il campeggio *campsite*
capisco: non capisco *I don't understand*
il cappuccino *frothy white coffee*
capricciosa: la pizza capricciosa *pizza topped with a variety of ingredients*
i carabinieri *police*
la caramella *sweet*
carbonara: alla carbonara *with eggs, bacon and pecorino cheese*
la carta assegni *cheque card*
la cartolina *postcard*
la cassa *cash desk*
il castello *castle*
la cena *supper*
cento *a hundred*
il centro *centre;*
il centro città *city centre*
che: che cosa? *what?;*
  a che ora? *(at) what time?;* che ore sono? *what time is it?*
chi? *who?*
chiama: come si chiama? *what's it called?*
chiami *call*
la chiave *key*
la chiesa *church*
il chilo *kilo(gram)*
chiuso,-a *closed*
ci: c'è *there is;*
ci sono *there are*
ciao *hello, hi; 'bye, cheerio, see you*
il cinema *cinema*
cinquanta *fifty*
cinque *five*
cinquecento *five hundred*
cinquemila *five thousand*

la cintura *belt*
la cioccolata *chocolate*
la circonvallazione *ring road*
CIT=Compagnia Italiana Turismo *Italian Travel Agency*
la città *city;*
  il centro città *city centre*
la classe *class*
la colazione/la prima colazione *breakfast*
come? *what?; how?;*
  come si chiama? *what's it called?;*
  come si dice? *how do you say (it)?;*
  come sta? *how are you?*
completo,-a *full*
compreso,-a *included*
con *with*
conservare *to keep, retain*
continua: permanente continua *no parking*
il conto *bill*
il contorno *vegetables (accompanying main course of meal)*
il controllo *inspection*
il coperto *cover charge*
coraggio! *good luck!*
corrente: la presa di corrente *electric point*
corretto: il caffè corretto *black coffee laced with brandy or grappa*
cosa: cosa?/che cosa? *what?;*
  cos'è (questo)? *what is (this)?;* cosa sono (questi)? *what are (these)?*
così *like this/that;*
  va bene così? *is that OK?*
la cotoletta (alla milanese) *veal cutlet in breadcrumbs*
cotto,-a *cooked*
crudo,-a *raw;*

il prosciutto crudo *cured ham*
la cucina *cuisine, cooking*

D
d'=di
da *from;*
  da bere *(something) to drink;*
  da cinquecento/mille (lire) *at five hundred/a thousand (lire)*
dalle (=da+le) *(+time) from . . .*
davanti *in front*
del (=di+il) *of the*
della (=di+la) *of the*
desidera?/cosa desidera? *can I help you?*
la destinazione *destination*
la destra *right;* a destra *on/to the right*
di *of*
dia: mi dia *(would you) give me*
dica: mi dica *can I help you?*
dice: come si dice? *how do you say (it)?*
diciannove *nineteen*
diciassette *seventeen*
diciotto *eighteen*
dieci *ten*
dietro *behind*
il diretto *train that stops at most stations*
la discoteca *discothèque*
dispiace: mi dispiace *I'm sorry*
divieto: divieto di sosta *no parking*
la doccia *shower*
dodici *twelve*
il dolce *dessert, sweet*
domani *tomorrow*
dopo *after*
doppio,-a *double*
dove? *where?*

dritto *straight on;*
  sempre dritto *keep
  straight on*
due *two*
duemila *two thousand*
il **duomo** *cathedral*

E

e *and*
è *he/she/it is; you are;*
  c'è *there is*
ecco *here (it) is, here
  (they) are; here you are*
ENIT=**Ente Nazionale
  Italiano per il Turismo**
  *Italian State Tourist
  Office*
l' **Ente Turismo** *Tourist
  Board/Office*
l' **entrata** *(f.) entrance*
espresso: il caffè
  espresso *black coffee*
l' espresso *express letter;
  limited stop express
  train*
estero,-a *foreign*
etrusco,-a *Etruscan*
un **etto** *a hundred grams*

F

fa: fa **caldo** *it's hot*
fame: ho **fame** *I'm
  hungry*
la farmacia *chemist's*
il faro *headlight*
favore: per favore *please*
la fermata *bus stop*
fermo: **Fermo Posta**
  Poste Restante
il fiammifero *match*
fino a *as far as; until*
Firenze *Florence*
firmi *sign*
il fiume *river*
fondo: là in fondo *down
  there*
il formaggio *cheese*
la fragola *strawberry*
il francobollo *stamp*

freddo: ho freddo *I'm cold*
freddo,-a *cold; iced*
il frullato *milkshake*
la frutta *fruit;* il succo di
  frutta *fruit-juice*
frutti: i frutti di mare *sea
  food*
il fruttivendolo
  greengrocer's
FS=**Ferrovie dello Stato**
  Italian State Railways
il fungo *(pl. funghi)
  mushroom*
funziona: non funziona
  it doesn't work

G

il gabinetto *toilet*
la galleria *tunnel*
gallese *Welsh*
la gelateria *ice-cream
  parlour*
il gelato *ice-cream*
il gettone *telephone token*
il ghiaccio *ice*
il giardino zoologico
  zoological gardens
il giorno *day;*
  buon giorno *good
  day/morning*
la gioventù *youth*
gli *the (m.pl.)*
il gorgonzola *gorgonzola
  cheese*
grande *big*
la grappa *type of strong,
  rough brandy*
grazie *thank you, thanks;*
  no, grazie *no, thanks;*
  sì, grazie *yes, please*
guardi! *look!*

H

ha *he/she/it has; you
  have;*
ha? *do you have?;*
ha bisogno di? *do you
  need?*
hanno *they have*
ho *I have*

I

i *the (m.pl.)*
il *the (m.sg.)*
in *in*
INAM=Istituto Nazionale per l'Assicurazione contro le Malattie *Italian National Health Insurance Service*
l' incrocio *(m.) cross-roads*
l' Inghilterra *(f.) England*
inglese *English*
l' ingresso *(m.) entrance*
l' insalata *(f.) salad*
irlandese *Irish*
l' Italia *(f.) Italy*
italiano,-a *Italian*
IVA=Imposta sul Valore Aggiunto *VAT*

L

l' *the (sg.)*
la *the (f.sg.)*
là *there;*
là in fondo *down there*
laggiù *down there*
lasci: mi lasci *leave me*
il latte *milk;*
al/con latte *with milk*
le *the (f.pl.); (+time) . . . o'clock*
le *(to) you;*
le piace? *do you like (it)?*
Lei *you*
la lettera *letter;*
la lettera raccomandata *registered letter*
il letto *bed;*
a due letti *twin-bedded*
il letto matrimoniale *double bed*
la limonata *lemonade*
il limone *lemon;*
al limone *with lemon*
la lira *(pl. lire) Italian unit of currency;*
la lira sterlina *pound sterling*

il litro *litre*
lo *the;*
lo stesso *all the same*
il locale *train that stops at all stations*
Londra *London*
lontano *a long way, far away*
il lunedì *Monday*
lungo: il caffè lungo *weakish black coffee*

M

la macelleria *butcher's*
il maiale *pork*
male: ho male *I'm in pain*
il manzo *beef*
il mare *sea*
margherita: la pizza margherita *pizza with tomatoes, mozzarella and oregano*
la marmellata *jam*
matrimoniale: il letto matrimoniale *double bed*
il medico *doctor*
meno *less;* meno . . . . . . *(minutes) to;*
meno un quarto *quarter to*
il menù *menu;*
il menù turistico *fixed-price tourist menu*
il mercato *market*
il metrò/la metropolitana *underground railway*
mezzo: e mezzo *half-past*
mezzo,-a *half;*
mezzo chilo/litro *half a kilo/litre*
mi *me;*
mi dica *can I help you?;*
mi dispiace *I'm sorry;*
mi piace *I like (it)*
mila *thousand(s)*
milanese *of Milan;* alla milanese *Milanese-style*
mille *a thousand*

la minerale/l'**acqua**
    minerale *mineral*
    water; una **mezza**
    minerale *a half of*
    mineral water
la minestra *soup*
misto,-a *mixed*
moltissimo *very much*
molto *very*
montata: la **panna**
    montata *whipped*
    cream
la mortadella *mortadella,*
    spiced pork sausage
la mozzarella *mild, rather*
    rubbery cheese
la multa *fine*
il museo *museum*

N

napoletano,-a
    Neapolitan
nazionale *national;*
    Italian
niente: nient'**altro?**
    anything else?
no *no;*
no? *isn't it?*
il nome *name*
non *not*
normale *2/3 star petrol*
la notte *night;* **buona**
    notte *goodnight*
novanta *ninety*
nove *nine*
il numero *number*

O

o *or*
oggi *today;*
oggi pomeriggio *this*
    afternoon
l' ombrellone *(m.) beach*
    umbrella
ora: a che ora? *(at) what*
    time?; che ore sono?
    what time is it?
l' orario *(m.) timetable*
l' ospedale *(m.) hospital*

l' ossobuco *(m.) knuckle of*
    veal
l' ostello *(m.) hostel*
ottanta *eighty*
otto *eight*

P

pace: in pace *alone, in*
    peace
paese: Bel Paese *mild,*
    creamy cheese
il palazzo *palace*
il pane *bread*
il panino *bread roll*
la panna *cream;*
la panna montata *whipped*
    cream
parla? *do you speak?*
il parmigiano *parmesan*
    cheese
il passaporto *passport*
la pasta *pasta; small fancy*
    cake
la pasticceria *patisserie,*
    cake-shop
il pecorino *ewes' milk*
    cheese
il pedaggio *toll*
la pelletteria *shop selling*
    leather goods
la penna *pen*
la pensione *pension, hotel;*
    mezza pensione *half*
    board;
la pensione completa *full*
    board
per *for; to;*
per favore *please*
perché? *why?*
perduto: ho perduto *I've*
    lost; mi sono perduto,-a
    I'm lost
permanente continua *no*
    parking
permesso? *excuse me,*
    let me by
la persona *person*
la pesca *(pl. pesche) peach*
il pesce *fish*

il **pesto** *sauce for pasta of crushed basil, garlic, pine nuts and pecorino cheese*

piace: le piace? *do you like (it)?;*
mi **piace** *I like (it)*
piacere *it's a pleasure*

la **pianta** *map*

il **piatto** *course;*
il se**con**do **piatto** *second/main course*

la **piazza** *square*

piccolo,-a *small*

pieno: 'il pieno, per favore' *'fill it up, please'*

la **pie**tanza *main course*

la **piscina** *swimming-pool*

più *more*

la **pizza** *pizza*

la **pizzeria** *pizzeria, pizza-restaurant*

un **po'** (di) *some, a bit (of)*

poi *then*

la **polizia** *police*

il **pollo** *chicken*

il **pome**riggio *afternoon;*
oggi pome**riggio** *this afternoon*

il **pompel**mo *grapefruit*

i **pom**pieri *firemen*

il **pomo**doro *tomato*

il **porta**foglio *wallet*

porto *I'll bring*

posso? *may I?, can I?*

la **posta** *post office;* **Fer**mo **Posta** *Poste Restante*

postale: l'ufficio **postale** *(m.) post office*

il **posto** *place*

il **pranzo** *lunch*

prego *not at all, don't mention it, any time; please do;*
prego? *can I help you?; sorry, what?*

prenda *take*

prendo *I'll take*

la **prenotazione** *reservation*

la **presa di corrente** *electric point*

presento *(may) I present/ introduce*

presto! *quick!*

la **prima colazione** *breakfast*

primo,-a *first;*

il **pronto soccorso** *casualty department*

il **prosciutto** *ham*

provare *to try (on)*

provinciale: l'Ente Provinciale Turismo *Provincial Tourist Board*

Q

quale? *which (one)?*

quando? *when?*

quanti,-e? *how many?*

quanto,-a? *how much?;*
quanto tempo? *how long?;*
quant'è? *how much is (it)?*

quaranta *forty*

quarto: e un quarto *quarter past;* **meno un quarto** *quarter to*

quarto,-a *fourth*

quattordici *fourteen*

quattro *four*

quattromila *four thousand*

questi,-a *these*

questo,-a *this (one)*

la **questura** *police station*

qui *here*

quindici *fifteen*

quinto,-a *fifth*

R

raccomandata: la lettera raccomandata *registered letter*

rallentare *to slow down*

il **rapido** *express train (inter-city type)*

la ricotta *kind of curd cheese*
il rilascio *issue*
il rimorchio *trailer*
il ristorante *restaurant*
il ritardo *delay*
ritorno: andata e ritorno *return*
Roma *Rome*
romano,-a *Roman;* alla romana *Roman-style*
rosso,-a *red*
la rosticceria *snack-bar/take-away*
la roulotte *(pronounced 'roo-lot')* *caravan*

S
il salame *salami*
la salsa *sauce*
il saltimbocca (alla romana) *veal escalopes cooked with ham and sage*
lo sciopero *strike*
lo scontrino *receipt*
scozzese *Scottish*
scusi *excuse me*
secondo,-a *second*
sedici *sixteen*
sei *six*
il semaforo *traffic lights*
semplice: l'acqua semplice *ordinary water*
sempre: sempre dritto *keep straight on*
senza *without*
sera: buona sera *good evening*
il servizio *service*
sessanta *sixty*
sete: ho sete *I'm thirsty*
settanta *seventy*
sette *seven*
settemila *seven thousand*
la settimana *week*
sì *yes*
siamo *we are*

la sigaretta *cigarette*
il signor ... *Mr. ...*
signora *madam*
la signora ... *Mrs. ...*
signore *sir*
signorina *miss*
la signorina ... *Miss ...*
singolo,-a *single*
la sinistra *left;* a sinistra *on/to the left*
SIP *(pronounced 'seep')* *Italian telephone company*
soccorso: il pronto soccorso *casualty department*
solo,-a *only, alone*
sono *I am; you are; they are;* ci sono *there are;* cosa sono (questi)? *what are (these)?;* che ore sono? *what time is it?;* mi sono perduto,-a *I'm lost*
sosta: divieto di sosta *no parking*
gli spaghetti *spaghetti*
la spiaggia *beach*
gli spiccioli *small change*
lo spogliatoio *changing-room*
la spremuta *fresh fruit-juice*
spumante *sparkling*
sta: come sta? *how are you?*
stagioni: quattro stagioni *four seasons*
stamattina *this morning*
stasera *this evening*
lo Stato *State*
la stazione *station*
la sterlina/la lira sterlina *pound sterling*
stesso: lo stesso *all the same*
la strada *road, street*
straniero,-a *foreign*

succo: il **succo** di **frut**ta
fruit-juice
sul (=su+il) *on the*
Suo,-a *your*
super *4 star petrol*
il **supermercato**
supermarket

T
la **tabaccheria** *tobacconist's*
la **tavola calda** *snack-bar*
il **tavolo** *table;*
al **tavolo** *at the table*
il **tè** *tea*
il **teatro** *theatre*
il **TEE**=Trans Europ Express
*trans-European luxury
express train*
telefonare *to telephone*
il **telefono** *telephone*
la **teleselezione** *STD*
tempo: quanto tempo?
how long?
la **tenda** *tent*
terzo,-a *third*
il **toast** *(pronounced 'tost')*
toasted sandwich
la **toilette** *toilet*
la **torre** *tower*
toscano,-a *Tuscan*
la **trattoria** *restaurant*
i **travellers** *traveller's
cheques*
tre *three*
tredici *thirteen*
tredicimila *thirteen
thousand*
trenta *thirty*
troppo *too much*
turismo: l'**Ente Turismo**
Tourist Board/Office
turistico: il **menù
turistico** *fixed-price
tourist menu*
tutti,-e *all*
tutto *all, everything*

U
l' **ufficio postale** *(m.) post
office*

un/**una**/un' *a, one;*
l'**una** *one o'clock*
undici *eleven*
undicimila *eleven
thousand*
uno *one, a*
urbani: i **vigili urbani**
town police
l' **uscita** *(f.) exit*

V
va *he/she/it is going;
you are going;*
va bene (così) *that's OK,
fine (like that)*
vado *I'm going*
vale *(it is) valid*
la **valigia** *suitcase*
vanno *they're going*
vedere *to see*
venti *twenty*
ventimila *twenty
thousand*
vero? *isn't it?*
la **via** *road, street*
il **viaggio** *journey;* buon
viaggio *bon voyage,
have a good trip*
il **viale** *avenue*
vicino *close, nearby*
i **vigili urbani** *town police*
il **vino** *wine*
il **vitello** *veal*
vuole? *do you want?*

Z
zero *zero*
zoologico: il **giardino
zoologico** *zoological
gardens*
lo **zucchero** *sugar*

English–Italian word list

A
a *un*
adult *l'adulto (m.)*
after *dopo*
afternoon *il pomeriggio*
  this afternoon *oggi pomeriggio*
agency *l'azienda (f.)*
  Local Tourist Agency Board *l'Azienda Autonoma di Soggiorno*
all *tutto,-i,-e*
alone *solo*
ambulance *l'ambulanza (f.)*
and *e*
annual list *l'annuario (m.)*
anything else? *nient'altro?*
as far as *fino a*
at *a*
avenue *il viale*
one *un, un', una, uno*
  one o'clock *l'una*

B
bag *la borsa*
bank *la banca*
bank note *la banconota*
bar *il bar*
bath *il bagno*
bathing hut *la cabina*
(to) be *essere*
  I am, you are, they are *sono*
  we are *siamo*
  he, she, it is *è*
(to) be *stare*
  how are you? *come sta?*
beach *la spiaggia*
bed *il letto*
  with two beds *a due letti;*
  double beds *il letto matrimoniale*
beef *il manzo*
beer *la birra*
behind *dietro*

belt *la cintura*
big *grande*
bill *il conto*
board *la pensione*
  half (partial) *la mezza pensione;*
  full *la pensione completa*
(from, of) Bologna *bolognese*
bottle *la bottiglia*
brandy *la grappa*
bread *il pane*
breakfast *la prima colazione*
(I'll) bring *io porto*
British *britannico,-a*
bun *la brioche*
bus stop *la fermata*
butter *il burro*

C
cake (small, fancy) *la pasta*
call *chiami*
campsite *il campeggio*
caravan *la roulotte*
cash desk *la cassa*
castle *il castello*
casualty department *il pronto soccorso*
cathedral *il duomo*
center *il centro*
  city center *il centro città*
change *il cambio*
(to) change *cambiare*
changing room *lo spagliatoio*
check *l'assegno (m.)*
check card *la carta assegni*
cheese *il formaggio*
  curd cheese *la ricotta*
  gorgonzola *la gorgonzola*
  mild, creamy *il Bel Paese*
  mild, rubbery *la mozzarella*
  Parmesan *il parmigiano*
  with ewe's milk *il pecorino*
chicken *il pollo*

child il *bambino*
chocolate la *cioccolata*
church la *chiesa*
cigarette la *sigaretta*
city la *città*
class la *classe*
close *vicino*
closed *chiuso,-a*
coffee il *caffè*
  frothy white coffee il
  cappuccino
  laced with brandy or grappa
  il *caffè corretto*
  small black coffee il *caffè*
  espresso
  weak black coffee il *caffè*
  lungo
  white coffee il *caffelatte*
cold *freddo*
  I'm cold *ho freddo*
cooked *cotto,-a*
cooking; cuisine la *cucina*
course il *piatto*
(second) (main) course il
  secondo piatto; la *pietanza*
cover charge il *coperto*
cream la *panna*
crossroads l'*incrocio* (m.)
cured ham il *prosciutto crudo*
cutlet la *cotoletta*
  veal cutlet in breadcrumbs
  la *cotoletta*
  alla milanese
current la *corrente*
  electric point (outlet) la
  presa di corrente

D
day il *giorno*
delay il *ritardo*
dessert il *dolce*
discothèque la *discoteca*
destination la *destinazione*
doctor il *medico*
double *doppio*
down there *là in fondo; laggiù*
(to) drink *bere*
  (something) to drink *da*
  bere

E
eight *otto*
eighteen *diciotto*
eighty *ottanta*
eleven *undici*
eleven thousand *undicimila*
embassy l'*ambasciata* (f.)
England l'*Inghilterra* (f.)
English l'*inglese*
entrance l'*entrata* (f.);
  l'*ingresso* (m.)
Etruscan *etrusco,-a*
evening la *sera*
  this evening *stasera*
everything *tutto*
exchange il *cambio*
excuse me *permesso; scusi*
exit l'*uscita* (f.)
express letter l'*espresso* (m.)
express train (limited stop)
  inter-city type il *rapido*
  l'*espresso* (m.)

F
far away; a long way *lontano*
fifteen *quindici*
fifth *quinto,-a*
fifty *cinquanta*
fill it up, please il *pieno, per*
  favore
fine la *multa; bene*
firemen i *pompieri*
first *primo,-a*
fish il *pesce*
five *cinque*
five hundred *cinquecento*
five thousand *cinquemila*
Florence *Firenze*
for *per*
foreign *straniero,-a;* l'*estero,-a*
forty *quaranta*
four *quattro*
fourteen *quattordici*
fourth *quarto,-a*
four thousand *quattromila*
from *da*
(in) front of *davanti di*
fruit la *frutta*

fruit juice *il succo di frutta;*
la spremuta
fruiterer *il fruttivendolo*
full *completo,-a*

G

gas bottle *la bombola*
General Delivery (Poste
Restante) *Fermo Posta*
(would you) give me? *mi dia?*
glass *il bicchiere*
(to) go *andare*
I go *vado;* he, she, you go
va; they go *vanno;* we go
(let's go) *andiamo*
good *buono,-a*
goodbye *arrivederci; ciao*
good day (morning) *buon
giorno*
good evening *buona sera*
good luck *coraggio*
good night *buona notte*
(have a) good trip! *buon
viaggio!*
gorgonzola *la gorgonzola*
grapefruit *il pompelmo*
greengrocer's *il
fruttivendolo*
grocer's *l'alimentari (m.)*

H

half *mezzo,-a*
half a kilo; liter *mezzo chilo;
litro*
half-past . . .*e mezzo*
ham *il prosciutto*
handbag *la borsetta*
(to) have *avere*
I have *ho;* he, she has; you
have *ha*
they have *hanno;* we have
abbiamo
do you have? *ha?*
have a good trip!; bon voyage!
buon viaggio!
headlight *il faro*
hello (hi) *ciao*
help *l'aiuto (m.)*
can I help you? *cosa*
desidera?; mi dica?*
here *qui*
here it is; here they are; here
you are *ecco*
hor d'oeuvres *l'antipasto (m.)*
hospital *l'ospedale (m.)*
hostel *l'ostello (m.)*
hot *caldo,-a*
I'm hot *ho caldo*
it's hot *fa caldo*
hotel *l'albergo (m.)* (plu. gli
al*berghi*)
how? *come?*
how are you? *come sta?*
how do you say? *come si dice?*
how long? *quanto tempo?*
how many? *quanti,-e?*
how much? *quanto?*
how much is (it)? *quant'è?*
(a) hundred *cento*
(a) hundred grams *un etto*
hunger *la fame*
I'm hungry *ho fame*
hunter's style (cooked with
tomatoes, onions and wine)
alla cacciatora

I

ice *il ghiaccio*
ice cream *il gelato*
ice cream parlor *la gelateria*
in *in*
included *compresso*
inspection *il controllo*
Irish *irlandese*
isn't it? *vero?; no?*
issue *il rilascio*
Italian *italiano,-a*
Italian National Health
Insurance Service *Istituto
Nazionale per
l'Assicurazione contro le
Malattie (INAM)*
Italian State Railways
Ferrovie dello Stato (FS)
Italian State Tourist Office
*Ente Nazionale Italiano per il
Turismo (ENIT)*

Italian Travel Agency
Compagnia Italiana Turismo (CIT)

J

jam *la marmellata*
journey *il viaggio*
  (have a) good journey! *buon viaggio!*

K

keep *conservare*
key *la chiave*
kilogram *il chilo*
knuckle of veal *l'ossobuco (m.)*

L

leather shop *la pelletteria*
leave me alone (in peace) *mi lasci in pace*
left *la sinistra*
  on the left *a sinistra*
lemon *il limone*
  with lemon *al limone*
lemonade *la limonata*
less *meno*
let me by *permesso*
letter *la lettera*
  registered letter *la lettera raccomandata*
(do you) like it? *le piace?*
(I) like it *mi piace*
like this (that) *così*
lira (Italian unit of currency) *la lira;* (plu. *lire)*
listen! *ascolti!*
litre (liter) *il litro*
(to) live *abitare*
London *Londra*
long *lungo*
look! *guardi!*
look out! *attenzione!*
(I'm) lost *mi sono perduto*
(I've) lost *ho perduto*
lovely *bello,-a*
lunch *il pranzo*

M

madam *signora*
map *la pianta*
market *il mercato*
match *il fiammifero*
may I? *posso?*
me *mi*
menu *il menù*
  fixed-price tourist menu *il menù turistico*
  Milanese style *alla milanese*
milk *il latte*
  with milk *al latte; con latte*
milkshake *il frullato*
miss (young woman) *signorina*
Miss . . . (formal address) *la signorina . . .*
mixed *misto,-a*
Monday *il lunedì*
more *più*
morning *la mattina*
  this morning *stamattina*
motorway *l'autostrada (f.)*
movie *il cinema*
Mr . . . *il signor . . .*
Mrs . . . *la signora . . .*
museum *il museo*
mushrooms *i funghi*
  with mushrooms *ai funghi*

N

name *il nome*
national *nazionale*
nearby *vicino*
need *il bisogno*
  do you need? *ha bisogna di?*
  I need *ho bisogno di*
Neapolitan *napoletano,-a*
nice *buono,-a*
night *la notte*
  goodnight *buona notte*
nine *nove*
nineteen *diciannove*
no *no*
not *non*
not at all *prego*
nothing *niente*

nothing else *nient'altro*
number *il numero*

O

o'clock *le* (plus numeral)
  eight o'clock *le otto*
of *d'; di*
of the *del; della*
O.K. *bene*
  is that O.K.? *va bene (cosi)?*
on the *sul; sulla*
only *solo*
open *aperto,-a*
or *o*
orange *l'arancia (f.)*
orangeade *l'aranciata (f.)*
others *altri,-e*

P

palace *il palazzo*
(no) parking *permanente*
  continua; divieto di sosta
pain *il male*
  I have a pain *ho male*
passport *il passaporto*
pasta *la pasta*
pastry shop *la pasticceria*
peace *la pace*
  leave me in peace (alone)
  —mi lasci in pace
peach *la pesca* (plu. *le pesche*)
pen *la penna*
pension; hotel *la pensione*
  half board *la mezza*
  pensione
  full board *la pensione*
  completa
person *la persona*
petrol *la benzina*
petrol *la benzina*
  2/3 star petrol *normale*
  4 star petrol *super*
pharmacy *la farmacia*
pizza *la pizza*
  topped with a variety of
  ingredients *la pizza*
  capricciosa
  with tomatoes, mozzarella,

and oregano *la pizza*
  margherita
pizza restaurant *la pizzeria*
place *il posto*
platform *il binario*
please *por favore*
(it's a) pleasure *piacere*
point *la presa di corrente*
police *la polizia; i carabinieri*
police station *la questura*
pork *il maiale*
postcard *la cartolina*
post office *la posta; l'ufficio*
  postale (m.)
Poste Restante (General
  Delivery) *Fermo Posta*
pound sterling *la lira sterlina*
(may I) present *presento*
pretty *bello,-a*

Q

(a) quarter *un quarto*
(a) quarter past *e un quarto*
(a) quarter to *meno un quarto*
quick *presto*

R

raw *crudo,-a*
receipt *lo scontrino*
red *rosso*
registered letter *la lettera*
  raccomandata
reservation *la prenotazione*
restaurant *il ristorante; la*
  trattoria
(to) retain *conservare*
return *andata e ritorno*
right *la destra*
  on (to) the right *a destra*
ring road (bypass) *la*
  circonvallazione
river *il fiume*
road *la strada; la via*
roll *il panino*
Roman *romano*
Roman style *alla romana*
Rome *Roma*
room *la camera*
round trip *andata e ritorno*

S

salad *l'insalata (f.)*
salami *il salame*
same *stesso*
  all the same *lo stesso*
sauce (for pasta, made of crushed basil, garlic, pine nuts and pecorino cheese) *il pesto*
sausage (spiced pork) *la mortadella*
Scottish *scozzese*
sea *il mare*
seafood *i frutti di mare*
season *la stagione*
  four seasons *le quattro stagioni*
second *secondo*
(to) see *vedere*
service *il servizio*
seven *sette*
seventeen *diciasette*
seven thousand *settemila*
seventy *settanta*
shower *la doccia*
sign! *firmi!*
single *l'andata; singolo*
sir *signore*
sit down *s'accomodi*
six *sei*
sixteen *sedici*
sixty *sessanta*
(to) slow down *rallentare*
small *piccolo,-a*
small change *gli spiccioli*
snack bar *la tavola calda; la rosticceria*
some *un po' di*
something to drink *da bere*
(I'm) sorry *mi dispiace*
soup *la minestra*
spaghetti *gli spaghetti*
sparkling *spumante*
(do you) speak *parla?*
square *la piazza*
stamp *il francobollo*
state *lo stato*
station *la stazione*
steak *la bistecca*

STD *la teleselezione*
sterling *la sterlina*
  pound sterling *la lira sterlina*
straight *dritto*
straight on *sempre dritto*
strawberry *la fragola*
  strawberry flavor *alla fragola*
street *la strada; la via*
strike *lo sciopero*
. . . style *alla*
  Milan style *alla milanese*
sugar *lo zucchero*
suitcase *la valigia*
supermarket *il supermercato*
supper *la cena*
sweet *la caramella*
swimming pool *la piscina*
(to) switch on *accendere*

T

table *la tavola*
  to the table *al tavolo*
take! *prenda!*
  (I'll) take *prendo*
telephone *il telefono*
(to) telephone *telefonare*
Telephone Company *SIP*
telephone token *il gettone*
tea *il tè*
ten *dieci*
tent *la tenda*
thank you *grazie*
  no, thank you *no grazie*
that's O.K. *va bene*
the *il, la, l', le, gli, lo*
theatre *il teatro*
then *poi; allora*
there *ci; là*
  there are *ci sono*
  there is *c'è*
these *questi,-e*
third *il terzo*
thirsty *la sete*
  I'm thirsty *ho sete*
thirteen *tredici*
thirty *trenta*
thirty thousand *trentamila*

this evening *stasera*
this one *questo,-a*
thousand *mille*
thousands *mila*
three *tre*
ticket *il biglietto*
ticket office *la biglietteria*
timetable *l'orario* (m.)
to (time telling) *meno*
  ten minutes to nine *le nove meno dieci*
toasted sandwich *il toast*
tobacconist's *la tabaccheria*
today *oggi*
toilet *la toilette*; *il gabinetto*
toll *il pedaggio*
tomato *il pomodoro*
tomorrow *domani*
Tourist Office *L'Ente Turismo*
tower *la torre*
Town police *i vigili urbani*
traffic light *il semaforo*
trailer *il rimorchio*
train *il treno*
  stops at all stations *il locale*
  stops at most stations *il diretto*
Trans European Luxury Express Train *Trans Europ Express (TEE)*
traveller's checks *i travellers*
(to) try on *provare*
tunnel *la galleria*
Tuscan *toscano,-a*
twelve *dodici*
twenty *venti*
twenty thousand *ventimila*
two *due*
two thousand *duemila*

U

umbrella *l'ombrellone* (m.)
underground railway *il metro*; *la metropolitana*
(I don't) understand *non capisco*
until *fino a*

V

VAT *Imposta sul Valore Aggiunto (IVA)*
(it is) valid *vale*
veal *il vitello*
  veal escalopes cooked with ham and sage *il saltimbocca (alla romana)*
vegetables (accompanying main course) *il contorno*
very *molto*
very much *moltissimo*
very well *benissimo*

W

wallet *il portafoglio*
(what do you) want? *che cosa (cosa) desidera?*
  do you want? *vuole?*
water *l'acqua* (f.)
  mineral water *l'acqua minerale*
  ordinary water *l'acqua semplice*
week *la settimana*
Welsh *gallese*
what? *che?*; *che cosa?*; *cosa?*; *come?*
  what are these? *cosa sono?*
  what is this? *cos'è (questo)?*
  what's it called? *come si chiama?*
  (at) what time? *a che hora?*
  what time is it? *che ore sono?*
what? *prego?*
when? *dove?*
where? *dove?*
where do you live? *dove abita?*
which (one) *quale?*
whipped cream *la panna montata*
white *bianco,-a* (plu. *bianchi, -e*)
who? *chi?*
wine *il vino*

with *con; ai; al*
  with lemon *al limone*
  with milk *al latte*
  with mushrooms *ai funghi*
(it doesn't) work *non funziona*

Y
yes, please *sì, grazie*
you *Lei*

(to) you *Le*
your *Suo,-a*
youth *la gioventù*

Z
zero *zero*
zoo *il giardino zoologico*

Panic stations!

You can hear how to pronounce most of these words and phrases at the end of Cassette 2.

Words you may need in a hurry

help!	**aiuto!**	listen!	**ascolti!**
let me by!	**permesso!**	look!	**guardi!**
quick!	**presto!**	look out!	**attenzione!**
call a doctor	**chiami un medico**		

When things go wrong

I've lost a bag	**ho perduto una borsa**
a suitcase	**una valigia**
a wallet	**un portafoglio**
I'm lost	**mi sono perduto,-a**
leave me alone	**mi lasci in pace**
it doesn't work	**non funziona**
I don't understand	**non capisco**
I'm English	**sono inglese**
do you speak English?	**parla inglese?**

In an emergency, telephone 113 **(centotredici)** and ask for

polizia	police
pompieri	firemen
ambulanza	ambulance

At a hospital, if you need the Casualty Department, it's PRONTO SOCCORSO.

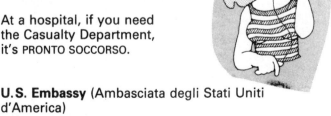

U.S. Embassy (Ambasciata degli Stati Uniti d'America)
119/a.v. Vittorio Veneto
Rome
Tel: (39)(06) 4674

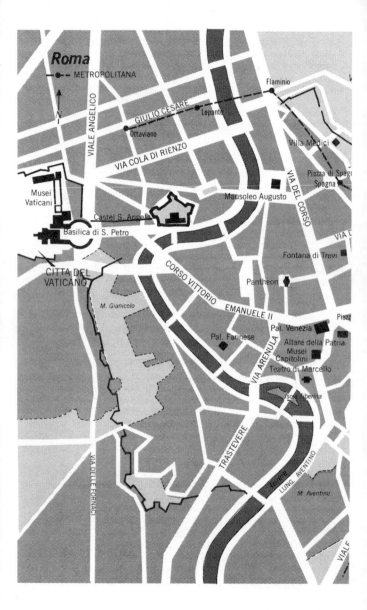

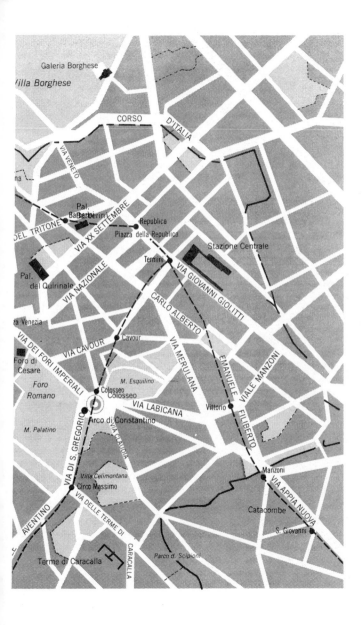

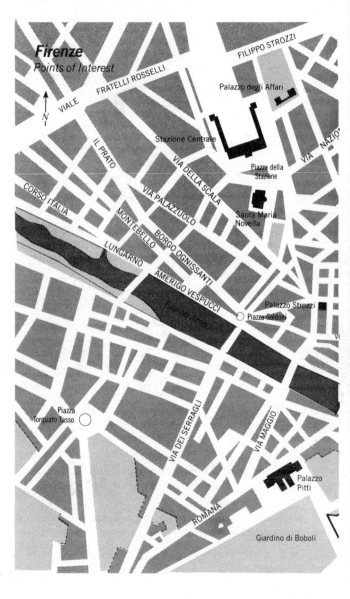

Firenze
Points of Interest

N

FILIPPO STROZZI

VIALE   FRATELLI ROSSELLI

Palazzo degli Affari

Stazione Centrale

IL PRATO

VIA DELLA SCALA

VIA NAZIO...

Piazza della Stazione

CORSO ITALIA

VIA PALAZZUOLO

MONTEBELLO

BORGO OGNISSANTI

Santa Maria Novella

LUNGARNO

AMERIGO VESPUCCI

Fiume Arno

Palazzo Strozzi
Piazza Goldoni

VI

Piazza
Torquato Tasso

VIA DEI SERRAGLI

VIA MAGGIO

Palazzo Pitti

ROMANA

Giardino di Boboli